New
Earth

by

Jack Chen

Southern Illinois University Press

Carbondale and Edwardsville

Feffer & Simons, Inc.
London and Amsterdam

Library of Congress Cataloguing in Publication Data

Ch'ên, I-fan.
  New Earth.

  Reprint of the 1957 ed.
    1. Hsin-têng, China (District)—Rural conditions.
  2. Collective farms—China—Case studies. I. Title. HN680.
  H7C5 1972   334'.68'310951   72–75332 ISBN 0–8093–0584–4

First published in March 1957 by the New World Press,
    Pai Wan Chuang, Peking
Preface and Postscript, Copyright © 1972 by Southern
    Illinois University Press
All rights reserved
Reprinted by arrangement with Jack Chen
This edition printed by offset lithography
    in the United States of America

To
Those Whose
Story I Tell

CONTENTS

LIST OF ILLUSTRATIONS

Drawings and Photographs by Jack Chen

PREFACE

This book describes how the 80,000 peasants of Hsinteng
County in East China's Chekiang Province freed themselves
from the poverty that still grips much of the world. By 1957,
practically everyone in the county lived in or did his work in
or through cooperatives: co-op or collective farms; handicraft,
credit and supply, and marketing co-ops. They were firmly
wedded to the idea of cooperation. It had served them well. It
had freed them from poverty.

The oppression and misery that formerly disfigured this
beautiful countryside were no more. The revolutionary armies
led by the Chinese Communist Party had freed them in 1949
from the inept and corrupt rule of Chiang Kai-shek's Kuomintang regime. Land reform gave the land to the tillers and by
cooperative efforts they raised the output of rice, their main
crop, by a third over the highest output before their liberation.
This was no mean achievement for six years of effort. For the
first time in history the whole county had enough to eat and to
wear. It was snugly housed. Illiteracy was being wiped out. Life
all around was better.

Hsinteng County is just one of China's 2,082 counties, just
one small part of a vast land in which historical and natural
conditions differ greatly from place to place. But it offers a
typical example of the socialist cooperative movement that has
swept the Chinese countryside. By 1957, almost all of China's
peasants were in semisocialist cooperative farms or socialist

collective farms. Eighty-three percent of them were in collective farms. This was the basis of China's Green Revolution. In 1949, China was a land of perennial droughts and floods, ravaged by pests and diseases, a land of constant hunger for the masses of the people. By 1957 it had virtually completed the socialist transformation of agriculture, industry, handicrafts, and commerce and brought its people to a state of relative well-being.

All this was part of the overall policy of socialist construction drafted by Mao Tse-tung, the gifted leader of the Communist Party. He had said in March 1949: "The scattered, individual farms and handicraft units which produce 90 percent of the total value of output of the national economy, can and must be led prudently, step by step and yet actively, to develop toward modernization and collectivization." He saw collectivization as the only path for a rapid, nationwide advance to prosperity for all.

China's 500 million peasants comprise over 80 percent of the nation. In a laissez-faire (free-enterprise) economy, their hundreds of thousands of scattered little farms could have formed the basis for the growth of private capitalist enterprise in China. But the policy of the Chinese Communist Party and People's Government, supported by the great majority of the people, calls for the socialist transformation of China's whole economic and social fabric. This demands that China's farms be brought together into collectives able to use large-scale mechanized and scientific methods of high-yield farming and make reliable, greatly increased contributions to unified state plans for food, handicrafts, and industrial raw materials. Step by step the Party has helped the peasants carry out this policy.

When this book was being printed for the first time in 1957, the peasants, not only in Hsinteng County, but throughout the country, were continuing to build up their collective farms. But they were finding that these were not large enough and lacked the resources to solve certain pressing problems. One collective farm might satisfactorily plan its own area for crops and distribution of manpower, but development of water conservancy (historically the basis of China's farming) and the necessary restructuring of the land, mechanization, and electrification, could often be handled efficiently only in cooperation with other collectives. For this reason networks of collectives farms were gradually set up to discuss and handle various problems in common. In 1958 one such network in Chayashan in Shuiping County, Honan Province, formally amalgamated to form the first rural people's commune in China. By the end of July that year, all 5,376 farm cooperatives in the Hsingyang region of Honan had merged into 208 people's communes. In August that year the Communist Party and People's Government gave their enthusiastic approval to this new type of collective farm and communes began to be established throughout China. Today all China's farmers including those in Hsinteng work and live either in people's communes or on state farms (see Postscript).

In a forthcoming book * I describe life and work on a rural people's commune in Honan Province. *New Earth* deals only with the growth of the co-op movement in Chekiang up to 1957. But a knowledge of how the collective farms were set up in China is essential for an understanding of the communes of today. This new edition of *New Earth* is therefore timely. It will, I hope, help to provide that knowledge. It appears at a time when world interest in China and the way things are done there is greater than ever before.

JACK CHEN

Honolulu, Hawaii
March 1972

* *Life in Upper Felicity.* New York: Macmillan, forthcoming.

NEW EARTH

Hsinteng county town

I

HSINTENG COUNTY

TO THE VALLEYS OF CHEKIANG

South from Peking, in January 1955, across the thousand kilometres of the North China plain. Hour after hour of bare, yellow soil, with nothing higher than some rounded hills to relieve its flatness. Across the broad flowing Yangtse at Nanking and on to Shanghai. Then southwest to Hangchow, the provincial capital of Chekiang. And the landscape is already more caressing. Verdant valleys, hills and mountains surround one; green gladdens the eye. Many fields already have the tips of winter wheat pushing through the black earth. But the weather is still extremely cold. Famed West Lake is a Chinese painting in white on grey. For the first time in twenty-seven years it is frozen over.

From Hangchow, southwest again, skirting the eastern shore of West Lake and up through a pass in the mountains. Small paddy fields in the breaks between the hills. Tea gardens on their slopes where the famous *Lung Ching* tea, the best green tea in China, grows. Then along the northern bank of the Chientang, with the river glittering below the road, junks with sails spread, long rafts of bamboos and pine, some, they say, from Hsinteng County, whither I am bound. Already I see the new sights of the countryside. Village smiths stand at forges glowing red

11

beneath new signboards: "Blacksmiths' Co-operative." In every cluster of shops I pass the busiest and most prominent are the consumers' or supply and marketing co-ops.

At Fuyang county town a crowd of girls, dressed in neat cadres'* uniforms and with sun-tanned, country faces, get on the bus. The badges on their jackets show they are health service workers.

Four hours' driving brings us to a long, broad valley, the centre of Hsinteng County. On either side, the bare, ribbed backs of the Tiehmu Mountains lie like a flock of sleek, sated dragons. We speed up a well-laid metalled highway lined with saplings, where only five years ago there was a dirt track "which," as a fellow passenger, a nurse, says, "you couldn't ride a cycle on in comfort."

In a few minutes, we reach the county town itself.

---

*The Chinese words *gan bu* literally mean a "person who works in a department," but today they mean much more than that. Workers of all kinds in revolutionary bodies, in government or Communist Party organizations, officials or staff of the trade unions, the various mass organizations such as the women's federation, the Youth League, the peasants' associations, in the co-operative movement, etc.—these are all *gan bu*. They do not like to be called "officials" because of the old connotations of this word, so translators have widely adopted the term "cadres" to describe them. I use this word too for want of a better one.

Hsinteng county town

COUNTY TOWN

When the People's Liberation Army freed Hsinteng county town in May 1949, it was an utter ruin. It was unscarred by gunfire. It had just slowly disintegrated in the years of Kuomintang rule. And in the last mad rush of defeat the Kuomintang troops had simply pillaged or destroyed anything that might be of use to the people.

The people's forces, the People's Liberation Army men and local guerilla fighters, took over the town. With them came a handful of young revolutionary cadres entrusted with the task of bringing order out of chaos. There was Comrade Chang, small, with a broad smiling mouth and keen eyes. A son of a poor-peasant family in Shantung, he had joined the revolution in 1946, worked in the underground movement in the Kuomintang rear for a year and then, when things got too hot for him, had been transferred to the guerilla forces. The next few years of his life were spent in constant campaigning. He had come south with the liberating army, doing organizing and propaganda work. Hsinteng would be his new home for many years. Then there was Comrade Chin, broad-shouldered, bluff, also a peasant lad who had been doing revolutionary work with the people's forces ever since 1946 in Shantung and other places. He felt a bit strange in this southern county with its unfamiliar accent. Here too was tall, bony Kuo, thirty years old, another poor peasant from Shantung, a revolutionary since 1947, a guerilla fighter, a political commissar, a brave man, straightforward as you make them, quick to take decisions. There were other comrades, trained by the Communist Party in revolutionary work with the people's army, men of the people who had passed through a searching school. They joined up with the local comrades who had come in from the guerilla units — about 60 cadres, armed. Forced up into the hills in their turn or lurking underground in the villages were a couple of hundred Kuomintang bandits and their agents: marauding Kuomintang stragglers and deserters, armed and desperate; hostile landlords barricaded behind their high-walled compounds and an assortment of rural riff-raff. The villages and the county town, with its hovels and ruins, gutters choked with garbage, steaming and stinking under the hot May sun, were terrorized by these desperadoes. But this was not the first time the cadres had faced the task of establishing revolutionary order.

After a few days the townspeople saw that there was no truth in the horrific rumours spread by the Kuomintang about the Communists. Life gradually resumed. At first it was much as of old. A few shops and stalls opened in the late morning and closed in the afternoon long before dark for fear of thieves. Two or three pedlars and a tea-shop completed the "business community." The one local mill had closed down for lack of fuel. There were only sixty-four pupils in the middle school, nearly all sons of landlords and rich peasants.

You must remember all this as you look at Hsinteng today. This is no garden town yet, but it is building, changing, seeing new things each year. No one wastes time imagining garden towns yet, but everyone is busy on the practical tasks and improvements that will surely build a garden town on this lovely site some day — and that day is not far distant.

It is already an attractive scene that meets your eye under a bright sun and a clean winter sky. The road from Hangchow is broad, well kept, with carefully tended fields spread on every side.

The low-pitched, red-tiled roofs of the new government offices and school for cadres contrast with the high white walls and black tiles of the former landlords' houses which have been repaired and requisitioned for the people's organizations. The battlements of the old confining town walls have been pulled down so that the town seems to stand on a terrace. Their stones are used to build new houses. Just inside the main gate you pass the co-op warehouse stacked with paper, charcoal and other peasant products. The streets are still narrow; rough cobbled, but clean swept. Several brand-new shops glisten with fresh paint.

The supply and marketing co-op, the prototype, as I later found, of others in every sizable village, has a full assortment of farm tools and farm furniture and all kinds of hardware. From the rafters hang skins of foxes, polecats, squirrels and deer caught by peasant hunters. Not many weeks ago, I was told, a famous hunter of the Chingho Collective Farm had sent in a six-foot tiger skin. Samples of fertilizer stand in great jars.

Next door is the large double-fronted state department store which is a replica of such stores in Peking, Shanghai or Hangchow. It too, like the supply and marketing co-op, stocks ready-made clothes, underwear, drapers' goods and haberdashery, toilet articles of all kinds, scented soap, many kinds of tooth-paste, a large selection of cotton goods, plain and printed, some silk and woollens and an extensive selection of stationery. There are many kinds of notebooks — a must for every cadre, co-op leader and schoolchild, and fountain-pens — a good-selling item. They say nearly half the young people here sport a pen, something undreamt of before. And if there's anything out of stock, it can be ordered. One co-op in Tungpu Township ordered and received eight cycles costing 150 yuan each. At that time the villages actually had priority over the towns for some industrial consumer goods. Prices are the same as in Peking, while some local products are even cheaper.

Next door, a big consumers' co-op also does a thriving business, supplementing the state store and giving it good socialist competition in service and prices.

There are several co-operative barbers' shops. They have their own sanitation code and the barbers wear white smocks and mouth-nose masks. Handicraft co-operatives sell all kinds of bamboo products, baskets, mats, chairs and blinds. One co-op is making the strong bamboo and oil-paper umbrellas for which the area is famous. The blacksmiths' co-op is mainly engaged on orders for the supply and marketing co-op. There are several sewing co-ops; one had a couple of dozen sewing-machines all whirring away, making clothes and silken banners for commemorative occasions and awards.

At the end of the street with that rather prim, quiet air of wholesale trade stands the government concern which deals in wines and cigarettes. There are many small shops and stalls selling its products retail or acting as agents for the supply and marketing or consumers' co-ops. There are several tea-shops and two really excellent restaurants. Hard by the old town gate is a newly decorated, prosperous-looking ironmonger's — a branch of a well-known Hangchow firm.

Nor must one forget the photographer who practises his esoteric art behind a modern shop front painted baby blue.

Every morning peasants gather at the informal marketplace at the crossroads before the supply and marketing co-op, with overflowing baskets. There are early vegetables, cabbages and bamboo shoots, sugar-cane and eggs and flat wooden tubs with the live ingredients of turtle soup in them. Fishermen have brought three-foot-long carp from the Fu Chun River and shrimps from the creeks. In the shops and stalls there are a hundred kinds of sweets, patties and cakes, rice dumplings and fried bean-curd in sauce, oranges, bananas and other fruit.

The New China Bookshop is a graphic chart of the intellectual growth of the peasants of Hsinteng County. Here you can find the classics of Marxism-Leninism, the works of Mao Tse-tung, books on agricultural science and farming techniques, on *How to Run a Mutual-Aid Team* and *How to Start a Co-op Farm.*

There is a counter full of one-act plays and ballads. Clearly the most popular are those about the co-op movement, its triumphs, trials and comedies. There are many picture books for those who are just learning to read; stories of People's Liberation Army heroes, of the revolutionary struggle, of the new Marriage Law and retellings of the ancient classics.

There are new editions of the great classic novels and translations from foreign languages. Practically every rural official I met had seen the film or read *The Gold Star Hero* by Babayevsky, that fine story of the co-operative farm movement in the Soviet Union. There is Ting Ling's *The Sun Shines over the Sangkan River* and Chou Li-po's novel *Hurricane* about land reform in Northeast China.

A blackboard outside gives notice of new books received: *Taiwan — Yesterday and Today* and *The Struggle for the Liberation of Taiwan.*

And between thirty and forty per cent of the buyers of these books are peasants.

All this thriving business was built up from nothing in the last five years. The greatest expansion of co-operative trade came last year following the announcement of the Party's General Line of policy for the advance to socialism and the campaign to expand the state and co-operatively owned sectors of the national economy and bring about the socialist transformation of the countryside.

And together with this new prosperity came other new things: clean streets, the dredging of the canal that runs through the town, new wells, new drains. A telephone service to Hangchow and beyond started in 1952. Electric lights went on in the main buildings. The county's mobile cinema team began to give regular shows in each district by turn. A new open-air public meeting ground and theatre was laid out and built. Periodic performances are

17

given here by professional groups from Hangchow and local amateur troupes from the surrounding co-op farms. A people's house of culture and a workers' cultural club with reading rooms, play rooms and free libraries and a mother-and-child welfare centre were opened. The radio diffusion centre was set up to transmit national and international news and local programmes to all the big co-ops. Today the middle school has 400 instead of 64 pupils. All the newcomers are sons and daughters of the peasants.

Hsinteng is a small town. As I passed down "Main Street" in my duffle coat, with sketch-pad open and camera slung round my neck, I must have looked the typical journalist. There were friendly and inquisitive comments but no one was much surprised — the press and visiting intellectuals are quite part of the picture of the countryside these days. Soon after I arrived I met a score or more of young artists from the Hangchow Art Academy, other journalists from the *Chekiang Daily,* and writers and playwrights from the Writers' Federation in Hangchow.

As I reached the lower end of the street I came to the privately owned Hsinteng Electric-Processing Mill. The young manager, standing at the door, gave me a cheery grin and invited me in. He was obviously glad to show his mill off. It mills husk for pig's feed.

"We couldn't make ends meet before liberation," he commented. "Finally we shut down completely. No petrol for the engines. Now we're working two shifts a day. We've installed a new engine and generator. We're making good profits and we're planning to expand operations shortly as a jointly operated state and private enterprise."

He was well satisfied.

Co-operation has changed the face of Hsinteng county town. The peasants in the market are fully and happily conscious of this. They think back to the rotten deals and fluctuating prices they got at the hands of middlemen and merchants subject to no law but their own — the crooked

18

law of the Kuomintang. They look at the bustling, lively reality of today where they themselves elect their deputies and participate in the running of their government, their county town and their co-operatives.

In the county town council they are discussing plans for the immediate future. They will turn the hill which rises over the town into a centre of local government and civic activities. New buildings will be raised here together with a better park, a playground for the children and a theatre. There are plans for a new public bath-house, for widening the main road, improving the lighting. . . .

Readers may find the accompanying chart useful in following events in Hsinteng County.

Government and Party Organization

in the

PROVINCE
People's Congress   Party Committee

COUNTY *(Hsien)*
People's Congress   Party Committee

RURAL DISTRICT *(Chu)*
Administrative Office   Party Committee

TOWNSHIP *(Hsiang)*
People's Congress   Party Branch

VILLAGE *(Chen)*

with

Party Branch or Group in Mutual-Aid Teams
or Co-op Farms

At the Paper-trough

NOTE ON THE COUNTY

Hsinteng County lies some sixty miles from Hangchow. It is half plain and half mountain, not a particularly fertile area, but well watered. The Tou, a small tributary of the Chientang, flows through it. This in turn has two tributaries, one from the northeast called the Sung Creek, the other the Golden Stream, from the northwest. The peasants pole rafts quite a way up these streams and they float timber down them from the mountain farms. There are regular roads from the highway with its truck transport and twice daily bus service to Hangchow, linked to paths for light push-carts and good trails for wheelbarrows leading right into the remotest mountain villages.

There are 18,000 households in the county with close on 80,000 people. Nearly all are peasants tilling the soil. Half the agricultural wealth of the place is in the rice crop, but there are fields too of wheat and vegetable oil, tea gardens, mulberry trees, and groves of bamboo which, besides being used to make paper, is turned into lovely baskets of many shapes and fans, umbrellas and furniture. Pine, cedar and other trees grow on the mountains. The peasants build their houses out of local stone and wood, eat their own rice, drink their own tea and enjoy their own fruit, pears, plums and sugar-cane. They sell these products too outside.

The peasants of Hsinteng have been making paper for many years. Today it is mostly rough stuff used for wrapping or toilet purposes, but there are many fine craftsmen, and fine papers are also being made. The pulp is made out of rice straw. This is first well rotted in lime and urine and then mashed by the hooves of water-buffalo going round and round in stone troughs sunk in the ground. For the finer grade of paper the pulp is mashed by foot-powered pestles in wooden mortars. It is then thoroughly washed by being put in specially strong linen bags and doused and squeezed again and again in a running stream. The blocks of pulp, looking like large blobs of reddish-yellow dough about as big as a pillow, are then carried to the paper-troughs.

These are usually set in friendly groups beside some water course and covered from rain and sun by rough shelters of bamboo and thatch. The pulp is diluted to the right consistency with water till it looks like thin brown coffee cream. A light frame of bamboo is immersed in this and withdrawn covered with a thin scum of pulp. The surplus water is allowed to run off and the film of damp paper — for that is what it is now — is placed to dry, sheet on sheet, beside the trough. When fairly dry it is peeled apart by women and the separate sheets put in the sun to dry. Finally the sheets are pressed flat and packed ready for the market.

The quality of the paper depends on the quality of the pulp and the fineness of the screen of the frame. The

21

best paper in Chekiang is made of rice straw pulped and processed with special care. In Hsinyen Village I saw a young craftsman making one of the finest screens available. Each strand was made of a single fibre split with painstaking care from the finest sort of bamboo — a fibre as slender as a hair. Such screens can be sold for a good price in Hangchow to make the high-quality paper Chekiang is famous for.

This rich diversity of products is one reason why the co-operative movement has developed here so rapidly. Various side-occupations — the most important of which is paper-making — provide some peasants with up to 40 per cent of their income. The need for better organization of labour throughout the year, for a more efficient division of labour between farming and cottage industries, is a real need that the mutual-aid team or co-op farm is well adapted to satisfy.

All these riches existed in the county before. But before the liberation, as I learnt in the weeks of my stay there, this was a valley of bitter suffering and want for the peasants. It is the land reform and co-operation which turned this natural wealth into houses and clothes for the peasants, with schools, books, good food and happiness.

Paper-troughs at Tumushan

IN THE OLD DAYS

This was one of the poorest of the eighty-one counties in Chekiang. The landlords and the Kuomintang, as they say, "drank the blood of the people." More than half the peasants were landless hired labourers or poor peasants owning less than a sixth of all its arable land. The handful of landlords and rich peasants owned more than half the land. The rest was clan or ancestral land or held precariously by the middle peasants who were constantly threatened with being thrown into the ever swelling ranks of the poor by drought, flood or civil war. Only a few managed to climb painfully and usually dishonestly into the circle of the few rich exploiters.

The landlords forced tenants to pay from 45 to over 70 per cent of the output of the land rented. They charged interest on loans of several hundred per cent a year. And to this they added the whole appalling burden of ruthless soldiery, police, secret agents, ignorance, superstition, corrupt courts, pressgangs, forced labour, and acts of rape and murder.

Not long after I got to the county I asked: "Weren't there any good landlords?"

The peasants looked up with eyes puzzled at the naivety of the question, but answered quietly: "No, only some who weren't quite so bad!" Could anyone be good who lived on the upper side of this press of exploitation? This landlord-Kuomintang slavery shackled the productive energies of the county. The mass of peasants were obliged to scratch a bare living from the soil with primitive implements and techniques. With hardly enough to keep body and soul together, starving sometimes for five months out of twelve, what was there to spare for buying fertilizer, better seed or tools? Even the peasants' spare time was robbed from them by the pressgangs or forced labour on Kuomintang military projects or in the landlords' houses. This was the life which the liberation ended.

young militiamen

LIBERATION

Liberation, however, was only the first act in a mighty effort by the peasants to emancipate themselves. The People's Liberation Army pursued the fleeing Kuomintang troops to the south. It was possible to leave only that handful of revolutionary workers to help consolidate the liberation of the county. But the forces of freedom grew like a snowball. Chang, Chin, Kuo and their comrades rallied the peasants to the Six Tasks proclaimed from the house-tops, posters on the walls and mass meetings.

The first was "Wipe out the Kuomintang bandits!"

Kuomintang saboteurs, Kuomintang troops cut off in the headlong flight of their army and landlord gangs, had taken to open banditry and terrorism against the villagers. These were hunted down by the security forces of the People's Liberation Army and the peasants' newly organized militia.

Several hundred of these rascals were rounded up. In Chinho Township, led by a single cadre from the county town, the peasants mustered all the weapons they had and went after the bandits themselves. They killed three, captured eighteen and the rest fled. (Two of these former bandits are now candidate members of the collective farm!)

Next, the "Anti-despot movement" mobilized the peasants against the worst rural tyrants and criminals who had oppressed the people. They were arrested, tried and jailed. Their property was confiscated and given to the most needy of their former victims.

Under the slogan of "Lower rents and interest rates!" the peasants at one blow put an end to the worst abuses — excessive rents and usurious interest rates. Meetings were held to bring these abuses into the open and mobilize the force of public opinion and revolutionary people's law against them.

Revolutionary order and security were firmly established. A great burden of rent (though not all rent) and debt charges was thrown off the peasants' shoulders. One by one the fetters of the past were shed.

The pattern of liberation unfolded further.

It was not the first time the peasants of Hsinteng County had risen against their oppressors. The stories of the great Taiping Revolution (1850-65) are still told in these valleys. It was drowned in the blood of peasants slaughtered by the vengeful landlords. There are reports of another rising, in recent times, when they seized the county town. Many peasants had learnt about a people's army and what the Communist Party stands for when the New Fourth Army had briefly come to these parts in the people's struggle for liberation. Many had joined to give it aid. So now things were different. The peasants' energies and ardour for freedom were led by a disciplined revolutionary party with rich experience.

They had a skilled and devoted guide with a tested chart of action. They became more fully conscious of the power of the organized people.

It was no wonder then that they responded with alacrity to the call of the people's government to "Pay the grain tax," the only tax that now remained of all the multifarious taxes and levies of the Kuomintang and the landlords. This amounted to only some 14 per cent of their crops in contrast with the 45 to 70 per cent which they had paid to the exploiters before.

They worked with new energy to fulfil the fifth task — "Raise production! Fight natural calamities!"

All this work and effort was inspired by the call issued by Mao Tse-tung, a name that was now on all their lips, "Organize!"

26

The handful or so of Party members in the county at the time of liberation had now gathered around them hundreds of peasants who had taken active and leading parts in the various campaigns. These formed the core of the new people's mass organizations. The peasants joined the peasants' association, women, the Women's Democratic Federation, the young people, the Youth League and Young Pioneers.

In the summer of 1949, the first peasants' conference was held, and in 1950 the first meeting of the first people's representative conference of the county.

The conference showed the reality of the people's unity: there were representatives of the workers of Hsinteng town, of the farmhands, the poor and middle peasants — the overwhelming majority of the county's population — handicraftsmen, the local merchants and business men, and intellectuals, the men of the People's Liberation Army, the women, youth, religious groups. They were united against those excluded from power — the feudal landlords and tyrants, the Kuomintang riff-raff.

These changes transformed the life of the people. There was now security, peace, stable prices, a reduced economic burden on the peasants — a real hope of better times. The people's power was firmly established. The county was ready to tackle the next task of the revolution — land reform to completely eradicate feudal landlord exploitation and all it stood for.

Ex-landlord's house built like a fort

LAND TO THE TILLERS!

The general facts about land reform in China are now fairly well known, yet every visit to the countryside, every question asked about this tremendous movement, brings out new facts of the unutterable cruelty, sordidness and mass misery which existed under the Kuomintang regime and which land reform ended.

Unrestricted power and greed everywhere brings out unbounded ferocity in those who exercise that power and are determined to continue indulging that limitless greed. The general picture of conditions in Hsinteng County is the same as elsewhere, but its details have special features.

In the county as a whole the landlords, numbering less than seven per cent of the households, owned or controlled over 60 per cent of the arable land. They owned nearly 30 per cent outright. (This amount is very considerably increased if mountain, forest and hillside pastures are taken into account.) The poor peasants, numbering 60 per cent of the households, owned only 16 per cent of the arable land. Land attached to ancestral temples or clans (over 30 per cent of the total area of arable land) was also in effect controlled by the ruling class of the villages.

In Chengling, a typical district, though the peasants here were perhaps poorer than elsewhere, landlords numbered only about four per cent of the households and owned or controlled 53 per cent of the arable land. The landlords were not good farmers. They didn't have to be — their income came from rent and usury. And they were not even knowledgeable enough to understand that a starving peasant is not the best of tenants. But then their logic was not ordinary logic. It was landlord logic.

28

The poor peasants, and hired labourers who often had no land at all, numbered 75 per cent of the households of Chengling District and owned less than 25 per cent of the land. Here, the ancestral or clan land, amounting to about 20 per cent, was also controlled by those who dominated clan councils, that is, the landlords or their agents.

The rich peasants who owned enough land, draught animals and implements and capital to engage in usury were only about two per cent, and the middle peasants something over 15 per cent of the households in Chengling District. The rest of the population was made up of handicraftsmen, pedlars, merchants, officials and a few workers. The total agricultural population was around 16,000 and the non-agricultural population around 1,700.

A poor peasant might have a *mou** or less of land and the right to till some of the temple or clan land by turns every two or three years, or at longer or shorter intervals depending on the amount of land and the number of persons who had to share it. The hired labourers usually had no land at all and no share in tilling the public lands. They suffered the greatest hardships.

The landlords exploited the poor- and middle-peasant tenants and the hired labourers. A peasant who wanted to rent land had to pay a substantial deposit on it for a start. Rents ran as high as 60 per cent and more of the crop. And it had to be paid no matter what difficulties were faced. On all the big occasions in the landlords' houses, such as births, marriages, feasts and deaths, tenant farmers and other "dependants" were forced to work for nothing at household tasks. On the other hand, when tenants celebrated they had to invite their landlords to their feasts, and at the big festivals send them suitable presents.

Bald figures cannot adequately give a picture of what this landlord yoke was like.

---

* One Chinese *mou* is about a sixth of an English acre.

Two knives are stuck in our back —
Rent and interest on our debts!
This load of misery is more than we can bear!

ran a peasant lament. Crushing rent, forced labour for the landlord and the Kuomintang and forced levies by grasping Kuomintang officials drove the peasants into a web of debt from which, in most cases, they found it impossible to escape.

If a poor peasant borrowed ten catties* of rice to tide himself and his family over the "spring hunger" when the autumn crop had been eaten and the new crop was not yet in, he would have to repay 20 catties, and sometimes more, within a few months.

The poor peasants and hired labourers were the main victims of the Kuomintang pressgangs. The *pao chia* heads (village heads) who "fixed" the conscription lists were all agents of the landlords. At the New Year festival the pressgangs were most active. They knew that men would be home to meet their folk then. A snowy beautiful clear moonlit New Year's Eve was their favourite hunting time. Snow would keep people at home and also show up the tracks of those who fled to the hills. New Year's Eve was also the time when the landlord pressed most relentlessly for repayment of debts. It was the traditional time of settlement of accounts, paying of wages and interest charges and repayment of debts. If you managed to hold off or avoid the landlord's summons that day you might well hope to keep him at bay for several months more!

> *Two knives are stuck in our backs!*
> *There are three ways out —*
> *Hang yourself,*
> *Flee from hunger,*
> *Go and get shelter in the jail!*

---

* One Chinese catty is 1.1023 English pounds.

In the winter when stocks ran out, the peasants ate rough grain mash, grass and any edible green thing. From October to February when the land was bare of green, they dug up grass and ate the roots which were still tender, or a hardy grass which sprouts in the fields low to the ground and is usually used to make green manure. In May and June they ate pumpkin. After the autumn harvest in July they ate potatoes and later rice for a month or two. But the rice crop was soon gone. Most of it was whisked away by the landlord and the tax collector as soon as it was harvested. Then the pots would be empty again.

> *Once you put away the sickle,*
> *Take out your begging bowl!*

Not twenty per cent of the people had good cotton-padded clothes for winter. Families shared clothes so that some could go out to work in the bitter winter cold — for Chekiang winters are sometimes almost as cold as in Peking. The women could not afford to wear long trousers, only thin stockings and trousers that came little lower than the knee. There were no stoves in the peasant homes. The ovens, heated with twigs or wood laboriously gathered on the denuded hills of the public domain, were lit only twice a day for meals in those houses where they could eat twice a day! — and this was the only heating. So they made little baskets lined with scrap metal, filled them with hot ashes and carried them to keep their hands and feet warm.

> *The landlord has his furs and fires*
> *To keep out the winter cold.*
> *We peasants wear ashes!*

In summer the peasant went barefoot or wore plaited sandals. In winter he wore wrappings of bark and bamboo fibre tied to his feet with straw twine. Many wore their hair long to keep their ears and neck warm, for they could not afford warm hats. It was not unusual, rather the reverse, for a family of five or six to share one cotton quilt. Some had used the same one for so long that they could not remember when they first got it, eight or ten or more years ago. Laboriously patched, washed and re-shredded, it became little more than a collection of waste cotton wadding and rags. Many didn't even have that, but used straw, paper, sacks or their raincoats of palm fronds to cover themselves at night.

The landlord's oppressive hand was felt everywhere, and at all times. It was felt too in the levies, pressganging and forced labour demanded by the Kuomintang government, for the Kuomintang government was also the landlords' agent. The landlords or their agents were the local government heads, village or *pao chia* chiefs or magistrates. And their cousins and relations filled the leading posts in the county, provincial and higher administrations.

The head of Shengyang Township, for instance, was a petty tyrant with four brothers, all of them in the Kuomintang. One brother was secretary of the Hangchow Municipal Government, another was a deputy *pao* head. Trained as a secret agent, he headed the local Kuomintang forces during the War Against Japanese Aggression, and exploited the people by pressganging them and forcing them to work for him for nothing. His wife was a landlord's daughter.

And this was not all. There was the "second root of poverty" — exploitation by the merchants and middlemen of all kinds. These, in collusion with the landlords and some rich peasants, monopolized the grain market and manipulated prices so that when the peasants came to sell their crops, prices were sharply depressed and when the peasants' grain stocks were exhausted and they needed to buy grain, prices were exorbitantly high. Similar tactics were used to rob the peasants of proper prices for the products of their side-occupations.

There was little chance of redress of wrongs inflicted by this tribe of exploiters because they themselves were judge and jury in any case brought against any one of them. The only limit to their oppressive acts was the ever-present fear that one day the peasants would rise, as they had often risen in the past, and administer summary justice for the crimes done against them. Landlords in these parts were still haunted by memories of the great Taiping uprising when the Heavenly Kingdom was established briefly and the peasants exacted bitter vengeance on their oppressors for centuries of criminal misrule.

The landlords' cruelty was somewhat curbed by that memory and the knowledge of what the peasants could do if they united under a resolute leadership to defend their interests. The reactionaries knew very well that when the peasants of neighbouring Kiangsi rose up under the leadership of the Chinese Communist Party, they took back their land from their oppressors. But sometimes their cruelty took the most bestial forms because the landlords hoped by this means to terrorize the peasants into such abject submission that they would never dare raise their heads.

There were few poor peasants who dared refuse the demand of their landlord for their womenfolk to serve in his house. Assaults on these defenceless women were frequent. Those who worked as servants were systematically ill-treated. One 12-year-old girl working in the house of the landlord Hung Men-chou was punished for a fault by being starved for three days. In desperation and hunger she stole food. When this "crime" was discovered Hung and his wife bound her and cut off her tongue.

Another 11-year-old girl, sent to gather firewood and staggering back through the house with a load weighing 40 pounds, accidentally knocked over and smashed a water pot. She was beaten within an inch of her life. As soon as she could move her limbs she ran away. But she was caught and brought back, forced into one of the great water jars of the mansion and scalded to death by the boiling water the landlord beast poured over her.

These are only two of the innumerable stories of land-lord depravity that emerged in the tragic "accusation meetings" that preceded the land reform when the peasants poured out the record of the horror and misery in which they had lived. It was at these meetings that they finally understood the stark need of ending the power of these brutes and the justice of returning to the people the land and goods that had been stolen from them.

By the end of 1950 the peasants of Hsinteng County had seen something of the power of unity in their various mass organizations. The people's power was firmly established. The bandits had been wiped out, the landlords "put in their places" and forced to reduce rents and exorbitant rates of interest. The first people's representative con-ference had been held. Here for the first time the people in council debated and decided on the affairs of the county.

Already a sizable body of reliable local cadres of the Communist Party, the people's government and mass or-ganizations had been formed. There were over 240 cadres at county, district and township levels with some hundreds of activists, the most resolute and active among the peasants and rural intellectuals, in the peasants' association, wo-men's federation and Youth League. When the provincial centre gave the go-ahead for the start of land reform they were all called together by the county Party committee. They made a thorough study of Party policy and the ex-perience of land reform gained elsewhere and in partic-ular one township of the county, Yungho Township, where land reform had already been carried out on an experi-mental basis earlier that year. Fourteen land reform teams were organized. The plan of action was laid out.

The land reform moved through four stages in fairly rapid succession from mid-November to December, a total of forty-eight momentous days.

In the first stage the policy was widely publicized among the peasants by meetings, by door-to-door talks, blackboard newspapers and plays.

Many of the peasants were still as though numbed by the years of oppression. Only by hearing others recount the crimes of the landlords and then thinking and speaking of their own fate themselves did they gradually see the real roots of their poverty and realize that as long as the landlords held their land and them in bondage, they could never be free, never begin the advance to prosperity. They finally grasped the idea that to make their liberation complete they must indeed *fan shen* — turn over — and throw the landlords off their backs.

In these meetings and discussions they also learnt how necessary it was to keep the landlords and their agents out of their organizations, out of the peasants' association in particular, since this was their mass organization for the carrying out of the land reform. Experience showed that the peasants' association must be "kept pure," that the farm labourers and poor peasants must form at least two-thirds of its leadership and that while they must work closely with the middle peasants, the latter, more likely to vacillate and compromise with the landlords, should not number more than a third of the leadership.*

This period of preparation and awakening and mobilization of the mass of peasants was extremely important and necessary because only the peasants themselves could carry the reform through thoroughly, only they knew all the intricate relations that existed in the villages, and could keep a vigilant eye on landlords and their agents to see that they did not sabotage the reform by hiding their land or goods from the people and suborning leaders of the movement.

---

*In Chengling District, poor peasants and hired labourers made up 5,288 of the 6,984 members of the peasants' association. They made up 720 of the 890 members of the people's militia and 245 of the 340 members of the Youth League.

In the peasants' associations, the peasants elected their own leaders for the work of land reform. They got great help from the work teams made up of local comrades from the county and many who came from the cities. These were led by experienced revolutionaries. They included workers from the bench and intellectuals who assisted in every way they could, giving guidance where it was needed, pointing out departures from policy, giving advice, helping with accounts, measurements and clerical work. Teams of cultural workers — artists, actors, musicians, ballad singers — helped with propaganda.

As soon as this stage of mobilization was completed a great conference of the peasants was held in the county town. The peasants' associations were now well established in the townships and they elected reliable delegates. The conference summed up what had been done and exchanged experience in dealing with knotty problems.

The conference delegates then studied one of the key problems of the next stage: how to differentiate between the various classes and apply the correct tactics to defeat all the counter-attacks and tricks of the landlords and their agents. The Party advised: Mobilize and rally together the farm labourers and poor peasants, the most exploited section of the peasants, as the resolute vanguard of the movement; unite with the middle peasants, drawing the most progressive into the leadership, rallying the wavering and the passive; neutralize the rich peasants who are potential allies of the landlords and often their junior partners in speculation and feudal exploitation; and direct the main blow squarely at the landlords — expose them! Organize public mass accusation meetings where their living victims can confront the landlords, accuse them of their crimes and show the peasants the concrete evidence and results of feudal landlord oppression.

The delegates then discussed the concrete situation in their villages. There was not a man among them whose family had not suffered hurt, loss or death because of the landlords.

It was this body of resolute, steeled men and women who returned to their villages and organized similar meetings there.

Landlords and their hangers-on were forced to attend in person. Face to face, the peasants accused them and asked the question: "Are you guilty?" Widows, orphaned children, emaciated, disease-ridden, crippled men and women gave the answer which some of these landlord tyrants were too malevolently angry to give — "Yes!"

Sometimes peasants feared to speak out even then against these criminals. In Hsinyen Village the people's militia had to bind the arms of the landlord nicknamed "His Fatness." Only then would the peasants speak out about their sufferings.

The peasants learnt to recognize their enemies and their friends, to see in their true colours those who had exploited and tormented them, and those who had suffered as they had suffered. Waves of sorrow swept these tragic meetings, waves of bitter hatred against the evil of all the past personified in the landlords who now stood for judgement before the people. But from these meetings the peasants went away with redoubled determination to sweep away this evil for good and all. "Turn sorrow and hate into strength!" was their cry.

The farm labourers, the poor and middle peasants became more united in this struggle. The middle peasants understood now that though they had not suffered perhaps as deeply as the poor peasants and labourers, they too had suffered from extortionate interest on loans, from high rents on the land they rented from the landlords, from other forms of landlord exploitation and from the general misrule of the Kuomintang as a result of which countless numbers of them had been thrown from their relative well-being as middle peasants into the ranks of the poor and vagrants. And for all of this, the landlords, the main prop in the countryside of the corrupt Kuomintang regime, were responsible.

It became clear to the middle peasants that their land would not be touched in the confiscation of the land of the landlords — that, in fact, those of them who had little land of their own but were forced to rent land from the landlords would actually receive land in the general redistribution. They became more whole-hearted supporters of the movement.

On the other hand, it became clearer to the poor peasants and labourers why they must make common cause with the middle peasants against the common enemy.

It was also made clear to the rich peasants that only those who had actually connived at and taken part in the landlords' crimes need fear the hand of justice. Only those would lose land who had surplus land, more than they themselves could till, which they rented out like feudal landlords. Those rich peasants who had nothing to fear from the land reform therefore were reluctant to make common cause with the landlords who were now the storm centre of the people's wrath and were being stripped of their power.

Now began a most important and difficult stage of the movement: the detailed class differentiation of the rural population.

General meetings of the peasants of each township, led by the peasants' association, classified all the peasants into groups: hired labourers and poor peasants, middle peasants, rich peasants, and landlords, industrial and commercial people and others (merchants, mill owners, pedlars, handicraftsmen).*

---

*In Chengling District with its 18,000 people there were only two industrial workers, 313 handicraft workers (exclusively engaged in their trade), 182 shop assistants, nine blacksmiths, three transport workers, and 216 people engaged in trade and commerce.

It was of the utmost importance to see that this classification was correctly made because it would determine whose land and property should be confiscated and who should receive a share of that land and property.

The policy was that the land, draught animals, farm implements and surplus grain of the landlords and surplus houses in the countryside should be confiscated;

that land owned by rich peasants and cultivated by themselves or by hired labour and their other properties should be left alone, but that, under certain conditions, land rented out by them might be requisitioned;

that land and other properties owned by middle peasants would be protected from infringement;

that land owned and used as part of industrial or commercial enterprises should be protected from infringement even though these were owned and operated by landlords.

In a word, the blow was to be struck mainly against feudalism and not capitalism, against the feudal landlords and no other class.

It was also laid down that in confiscating, requisitioning and distributing the land the township should be taken as the basic unit. It should be distributed in a uniform manner, according to the population in that township, on the principle of allotting the land to its present tiller, while making adjustments in land-holdings by taking into consideration the amount, quality and location of the land. The landlords and their families too would be given an equal share of land so that they could make their living by their own labour and reform themselves through honest toil.

Another peasant conference was held in the county town to review the work done, pass on experience and study the next step: the actual confiscation of the landlords' land and property, and its distribution.

Experienced revolutionary workers checked over the lists classifying the peasants, consulted the land deeds preserved in the county from the past, and helped the peasants' associations correct any mistakes.

It was found that this difficult task of class classification had been well carried out throughout the county. All who wished had been invited to contest disputed points before the higher authorities in the districts and county. There were few challenges when the final lists were posted up in the villages. At every step the people had been thoroughly consulted and had had the final word. As the peasants say: "The masses have sharp eyes!"

On the return of the delegates from the county town, each township set up its confiscation and distribution committees. The most trusted and tried, those known for their firm stand in defence of the people, for their honesty and incorruptibility, were elected to serve on it. Under strict democratic control, the land, livestock, farm equipment, surplus grain and certain other property of the landlords were confiscated and stored. The results of this too were reported to, summed up and studied at a county conference of peasants. Then the distribution started.

The distribution committees in consultation with the peasants made out the plan of distribution. They studied exactly what was available for sharing out and what were the needs of the peasants. Each household was asked to report exactly what it already possessed and what its needs were. They were called upon to preserve comradely unity, considering the needs of others as closely as their own. Only when all were satisfied were the final lists posted up showing who should get what. Then the actual distribution began.

On that great day in Chengling District all the 272 households of farm labourers with their 467 members received land amounting to 445 *mou*. The 3,000 poor-peasant households with over 10,500 members received a total of over 9,000 *mou*. 481 middle-peasant households received nearly 1,000 *mou*. (Even some rich peasants received land which they had formerly rented.) It worked out at from one and a half to two *mou* a head.

Over 140 buffaloes, 1,320 rooms and over half a million catties of grain were distributed. The poor peasants and hired labourers received 84 ploughs, 75 harrows, 740 hoes, 145 water-wheels, 100 threshers, 135 buffaloes, 830 rooms and most of the grain.

All this of course was not accomplished without acts of revenge or attempted sabotage on the part of the landlords. They tried directly, or through their agents and hangers-on, to create distrust between the peasants and their leaders. In Hsinyen Village the local landlord used a rich-peasant agent to stir up the villagers with stories that Chen Ching-chao, a middle-peasant activist, was making improper use of confiscated goods. They surrounded his farm-stead and there was a tense and bitter moment until the matter could be explained. It finally ended in the exposure of the landlord rumour-monger.

Landlords tried to conceal their property. They spread rumours that "the U.S. Army has crossed the Yalu! Chiang Kai-shek will soon be back!" Landlord Ho Pei-fu of Chin-shan Township in a fury set fire to his own house to prevent it from falling into the hands of the peasants. In a final fit of impotent rage another went down on the morning after the land distribution, tore out markers giving the names of the new owners and ran his plough in crazy furrows across the fields. Others tried to bribe officials or activists with promises of money or even their daughters' hands in marriage. Shots were fired out of the night at peasant leaders.

The peasants handed the criminals they caught to the people's courts to deal with. Notorious murderers faced severe punishment, those guilty only of the "ordinary" forms of exploitation and crime were put under surveillance, allowed to work on their land and turn themselves into honest citizens. The landlords were told that they could regain their civil rights after a few years if they behaved themselves properly.

The mercy granted to these scoundrels by the people in their hour of victory contrasted vividly with the ruthlessness of their oppressors in the past. Men who had been guilty of years of pitiless exploitation, of driving people to death, of breaking up families, of keeping the mass of the people in ignorance and starvation, were given land, virtually pardoned and urged to make themselves into decent human beings.

One who was recently released from imprisonment felt too ashamed to come back to the district and went to settle in another place. Another wrote recently to his relatives that he had become a "model prisoner," an expert at basket-weaving, and would soon be released before his time. Today most are back at home working contentedly in the collective farms!

In the villages I found that the peasants act scrupulously on the principle that it is "as a class" that the feudal landlords must be wiped out. Once the individual landlord has given up his way of life — which is inherently a criminal way of life — and sincerely determines to make amends for the past, that is, gives up his class position and disarms himself, then, while proper vigilance is exercised, everything is done to win him back as a useful member of society. The law is that he and his family must suffer no unwarranted hurt.

On one occasion, for instance, when as we were passing a house and it seemed possible that our discussion of the events of the land reform might be overheard by members of the landlord's family within, a cadre and peasant simply cut the conversation short until we were out of earshot.

And so the peasants, celebrating their victory with that gentleness that I found on every side, were satisfied that strict justice, tinged wherever possible with mercy, should be meted out to their enemies.

Great mass meetings and parades were held in all the 32
townships to celebrate completion of the land reform. The
peasants brought out the fruits of their victory. They
paraded with their new buffaloes and ploughs, hoes and
other implements. The animals were decorated with large
red rosettes. Huge banners proclaimed:

Land and animals back to the tillers!
Now we've got water-wheels, we've no fear of drought!
Now we've got ploughs, we can raise more grain!
We've stood up! We'll never forget the Communist Party!
*Now we're victorious, we'll never forget the People's
Liberation Army!*
Three cheers for the Communist Party!
Long life to Chairman Mao Tse-tung!

In Sungyen Township, 1,500 people joined a five *li* long
procession through the villages and fields. To the music of
drums and cymbals they danced the *yangko,* the spirited
festival dance that had come to the district with the People's Liberation Army from the north, from Yenan.
Seventy-year-old Hsu and old Mrs. Pan, the "model de-
pendant" of a PLA fighter, danced, the whole township
danced!

That year they delivered their grain in long lines of gaily
decorated carts and wheelbarrows with great banners
streaming overhead and bands leading the way, calling it
"Victory Grain" and "Grain from the Great 'Turn Over'!"

It was at that time that the call went out to "Resist
American Aggression and Aid Korea!" The American army
was advancing to the Yalu. Almost every able-bodied
youth of the county volunteered though few were actually
accepted for service in Korea. Peasant women, who had
never been more than a few miles from their homes all
their lives, volunteered, saying: "We'll cook and sew for
the Volunteers!"

Though it was a bitterly cold winter, everyone wanted to get to work. Almost every able-bodied man in Chengling District contributed forty workdays to the digging and building of the Takuang Pond and the Kwangshan Reservoir that, when completed, held enough water to irrigate 11,000 *mou* of land. The people's government insisted that they should each take a receipt for work done with the right to claim compensation later.

In the spring of that year, 1951, the mutual-aid movement developed apace. Many work-exchange groups and mutual-aid teams were organized.

The peasants sang a new song:

Before we lived in Hell!
Now we're up in Heaven!

A farmstead—

II

UNITE FOR PROSPERITY!

FIRST STEPS — WORK-EXCHANGE GROUPS

But now we must go back a bit if we are to understand how the peasants put their feet on the first rungs of the ladder of co-operation.

In the spring of 1950 — eight months after liberation and even before the land reform — some work-exchange groups were formed. It came about this way.

Spring sowing in Hsinteng County has to start in March, but the peasants were faced by many difficulties. It was only a few months after liberation. The last orgy of pillage and pressganging by the Kuomintang had left the peasants with most of their reserves exhausted. Some families which had lost sons or husbands in the wars were without rice-winners. The summer of 1949 had been exceptionally rainy and the crops had suffered: some were washed out by flooding rivers and freshets, others were water-logged and spoilt. There was a lot of work to do and it had to be done speedily. Some of the most needy peasants had already received the land of convicted tyrants, but most important, they, like many others, lacked seed and tools to cultivate their land.

This was the case in Hsinyen Village in Sungyen Township, so it was natural that the peasants should fall back on the age-old tradition of neighbourly help to get over pressing difficulties. In the old days this had usually been a matter of close neighbours or relations helping each other, and not infrequently the economically stronger partner would insist on getting the better of the exchange, family relationships notwithstanding. It was also the custom for the various partners to exchange meals as they worked on each other's land. This was a heavy burden on the poor peasants.

But now a new spirit animated these groups. The new conditions created by liberation and the guidance given by the Communist Party immediately brought about a change in the old pattern of such mutual aid. They were organized on a wider scale than ever before. The peasants naturally wanted to do what they could particularly to help the families of those whose rice-winners had lost or sacrificed their lives in the revolution and the War of Liberation. A new spirit of comradeship was abroad. The Party popularized the slogan "All peasants are brothers!"

In Hsinyen Village it was a poor peasant, Hsu Kuei-yung, who took a lead in this.

Hsu is middle-aged with a keen, humorous face, wrinkled it seems as much by old worries as by laughter. He has a wife, today comfortably housewifely, a bright little girl of fourteen and a son, aged nine. His old father, nearly 70, is still working. They live in a four-roomed cottage built by the old man on a small patch of ground by the paddy fields. They had no land but had bought a buffalo calf and had scrimped and saved and reared it to hire out so that it represented nearly half their wealth. Hsu was a useful man to exchange work with.

Hsinyen Village is hard by the Chengling district Party centre, so it was not long before Hsu was close friends with the comrades there. Chin, whom we met first in the county town, was now Chengling district Party secretary. Like the other comrades from Shantung, he had had experience of such work-exchange teams in the old liberated areas of the

46

north, so he could give valuable advice. Hsu Kuei-yung brought his troubles to him.

"First of all, those families who haven't much labour to exchange don't have such an easy time of it. Next, everyone is expected to bring his own big implements and some haven't got any. And sometimes it's more like meal exchange than work exchange! A man gets a meal no matter how he works!"

The Shantung comrades advised Hsu and others who had similar difficulties to end the burdensome exchange of meals altogether and see that the principle of mutual benefit was more strictly observed. The Hsinyen team was better organized too. Team members were roughly divided into "full manpower" and "half manpower" for purposes of assessment of exchanges. (One with "full manpower" was one who could till up to ten *mou*.) So a family with two "half manpowers" could exchange equitably with a "full manpower" and no hard thoughts. Then instead of the whole group going to do a job, as they had in the past, a leader was elected for the season and he decided in advance just how many hands were needed for a particular job. A hiring fee was paid for animals and large implements like ploughs or harrows.

These better teams were organized at first mostly on the outskirts of the county or district centres. Gradually more and more villages followed their example and they became generally popular. The good feeling engendered by liberation did much to iron out difficulties.

In Chengling District over 250 work-exchange teams were formed and worked through the autumn of 1949 and the spring and autumn of 1950. But not all were as well organized as they should have been and not all were entirely voluntary. This was frankly recognized as a defect, tolerated for the moment because in some places the emergency demanded the formation of such groups by administrative order as a relief measure. Individual cases of dissatisfaction naturally occurred in such teams. Owing to inexperience there were cases where implements and animals used were not equitably paid for so that the peasant owners objected. In many cases, of course, the owners were middle peasants and this was particularly regrettable in view of the importance of the policy of fostering close unity between the poor and middle peasants. Such groups were naturally less stable than the completely voluntary ones.

These points were carefully noted by the Party workers and peasant activists when they reviewed their work in the spring of 1950. They used the experience gained to turn certain of the best groups and teams into models and pioneers for the movement. Some of these teams later became famous co-operatives in the county. The teams led by Yang Yu-chuan, Hsiung Chin-shao and Hsu Kuei-yung were then some of the best of them.

When the famous Shansi mutual-aid team leader and model peasant, Li Shun-ta, sent out a nation-wide call for greater production to help the nation, these work-exchange teams sparked a response from the entire county. By the end of 1950, 75 per cent of the households of Chengling District, the leading district in the county, were organized into such teams and were taking part in an emulation movement, the first in the history of the county.

The teams were seasonal affairs. All but 96 out of 725 in the county dissolved after the autumn harvest. But they gave a good account of themselves. Inspired by the liberation, buoyed up by the knowledge that the land they tilled would soon be made theirs by the coming land reform, members of well-organized teams got yields of 330 catties of rice per *mou*. This was more than 10 per cent above the average yields got in 1949, the last pre-liberation harvest. The "spring hunger" that was a commonplace under the Kuomintang was thus wiped out within a year of the people taking power.

The work-exchange teams, simple as they were, demonstrated what could be achieved by mutual aid among emancipated peasants.

SEASONAL MUTUAL-AID TEAMS

After the land reform in the winter of 1950-51, the peasants of Hsinteng County jubilantly surveyed the fields they now owned, rent free and debt free. With unparalleled enthusiasm they grappled with the immediate practical tasks that faced them.

The spring sowing was due. There were many old and new problems to be solved. Most peasant families still lacked enough manpower or tools to do the work thoroughly on their own. Some indeed had many work hands but not so much land; others had many small mouths in the family and therefore large fields (for even the babies got a share of land in the land reform), but few work hands. Some had bamboo groves and tea gardens and didn't know how to care for them or couldn't. Some had hoes, but no ploughs or animals. Some had ploughs but not much land to use them on. It was only natural that they should all look again to mutual aid to solve their problems.

But now the work-exchange teams or, as the better-organized ones were called, seasonal mutual-aid teams, were formed on the new social basis created by the land reform.

Landless hired labourers of yesterday now had land and were eager to put their strength and brains into these joint endeavours. Organized together with the poor peasants, they were able to guide the teams and influence their middle-peasant friends in the right direction, by preventing, for instance, the economically stronger members of teams from taking undue advantage of their position. The Party members too were able to bring to their guidance the results of fresh nation-wide experience which the central

Party organizations had collected from branches all over the country and sifted and summarized.

The local Party leadership particularly stressed that the principles of voluntariness and mutual benefit must be strictly observed. Also, since several local cases of bossiness in running the teams had been observed, they added the advice to team leaders to pay particular attention to working out ways of democratic management. "Socialism can't be built by giving orders," they warned.

With the immediate emergency over, all the administratively organized work-exchange teams were dissolved and rebuilt on a voluntary basis. Thus, by the time of the spring ploughing the 250 work-exchange teams of the year before in Chengling District had been reorganized into 720 smaller teams more conveniently sited and based on the peasants' own choice of partners and ability to organize. Later, in the autumn of 1951, a further reorganization of teams took place. By this time Chengling District had some 450 of the improved work-exchange teams or seasonal mutual-aid teams, and in the county elections for the best teams it did well. Hsu Kuei-yung's team was cited as a model and many peasants came to see how it worked.

These new seasonal mutual-aid teams were usually formed with between half a dozen and a dozen households. All took it for granted that land and implements, seed, fertilizer and so on were privately owned. The farmers came together only for jointly managed labour at busy seasons, for the rest of the time they engaged in individual labour whether in the fields or at side-occupations, and of course the harvest was theirs to dispose of as they wished after paying the agricultural tax.

When the time came for joint work, such as sowing, transplanting or harvesting, the team decided on the order in which the fields should be worked. This was always a touchy question, especially in new teams, for early ploughing, sunning, and sowing of the fields meant higher yields.

If the buffalo used belonged to a team member a fixed tariff was agreed upon. This was paid by the owner of the land on which it was used. The mutual-aid team then selected its best ploughman. He was credited with a day's work or more and the landowner repaid this either in labour during the season or its equivalent when accounts were totted up (at the wage rate prevailing in the district).

The Party spread the experience of the model teams. Methods of assessing labour by a points system were introduced, a great improvement on the work-exchange group's "full-manpower, half-manpower method." The best method used was the "fixed points flexibly applied" or "variable assessment" method. A good, strong worker was assessed at, say, ten points, while a weak one was assessed at, say, five or six. But if the ten-point man didn't do his best on a particular day the team credited him with less points while the six-point man, if he did extra well, was credited with extra points.

This system was used in the best seasonal mutual-aid teams and even some permanent or year-round mutual-aid teams, for some of the best seasonal mutual-aid teams were already pressing ahead to this higher form of co-op organization. It should be remembered that throughout the period under discussion the movement for co-operation was in a constant state of advance and sometimes a work-exchange team might be using good methods discovered in a seasonal mutual-aid team while later a permanent mutual-aid team might be using improvements discovered in a farming co-operative, a still higher form of co-operation.

Big increases in yield resulted from the better organization of labour in these seasonal mutual-aid teams. The best man could be used for a job; labour was encouraged by fairer assessment of efforts and therefore fairer pay; there was a big advance in the political consciousness of their members bound together now by comradely ties and not by mere urgency or administrative order. The new spirit of the peasants following the land reform had a lot to do with it too.

In the seasonal mutual-aid team at Hsu Kuei-yung's village, one of the best at this stage, yields of 400 catties per *mou* were being got compared with 320 catties per *mou* in the work-exchange group stage.

By this time too the Party organization was being improved and strengthened in the area and the apparatus of the people's government was working more and more efficiently. Young and old officials were shaking down in their jobs at the various levels of administration — the township (*hsiang*), district (*chu*), county (*hsien*) and province.

Today every district and township in the county has its Party committee or branch, and there are many groups or sub-groups (with a minimum of three members) in the hamlets, the mutual-aid teams and co-op farms. Everywhere (for this county is entirely agricultural) their main work is to give day-to-day leadership to the co-op movement, not only by precept and education, but on the farms, by their own example as model farmers and organizers. So each group of Party members, no matter how small, has become a dynamo, powering the co-op movement in its locality. Each branch works hard to make its township a model in the movement. Regular meetings held in the district and county play a big part in checking up work and passing on experience from one branch to another.

As we know there was only a handful of Party members in the county centre at liberation. It is one of the big achievements of the Party that here, as elsewhere, it has rallied round it and trained a new detachment of staunch Communists from among the most resolute of the peasants, men and women who are taking the lead in the advance of the peasants to socialism. Today these new peasant leaders hold responsible posts in the township, district and county Party offices, people's government administrations, and mass organizations.

Besides having this "grass roots" leadership and organization, the Party also ensures that its leading organizations at every level have close contacts with the movement. Each committee or branch takes part in the practical day-to-day work of one or other of the lower organizations. Thus the Chekiang provincial committee has a "key" county under its direct guidance (in this case Hsinteng County). The county and district committees in turn each have "key" districts and townships under their direct care. The Chengling district committee, for instance, has Sungyen Township as its special care. To this it takes the general directives of the Party on the co-op movement, and, on the spot, in direct contact with the actual situation there and with the local Party members, it helps to work out ways and means of carrying them out. On the other hand, it carries the results of its own practical experience as well as that of the other branches under its general direction to the higher organizations, up to the central organization of the Party, for summarizing and generalizing and providing not only immediate, but long-term guidance for the movement. Then this sifted experience goes back again for the concrete guidance of the peasants in its own and other districts. This process goes on constantly at every stage and level of the movement. It is a constant check of theory against experience and experience against theory. This exemplifies the method of "from the masses, to the masses" so brilliantly summarized by Chairman Mao Tse-tung for the guidance of the Party in his directive "On Methods of Leadership."* Thus there are always pioneer mutual-aid teams and co-op farms going ahead of the general advance and serving as pathfinders or experimental grounds for the movement. Their good points are popularized throughout the county. Their defects serve as a warning of what to avoid.

* "On Methods of Leadership," *Selected Works of Mao Tse-tung,* Vol. IV, Lawrence & Wishart, London, 1956.

There is also the direct and indirect guidance of the higher levels of the Party. Regular directives are sent down, summing up national experience. Leading members of the Party regularly visit the localities to see things for themselves and take part in the work there. The heart-beats of the peasants are truly heard in Peking.

And all the time, as the mass movement develops, groups of activists, the best and most active representatives of the peasants, are rallied round the Party to be nurtured and trained and tested as revolutionary workers of the people. So today the 60 Communist Party members in the county at the time of the liberation have grown to over 300, with 2,000 Youth League members and hundreds of other activists.

It goes without saying that the peasants elect as deputies to their people's congresses those who take the lead in village affairs and that means in the co-op movement that remarkable school of democracy.

This is of course only a very sketchy description of an intricate process, but it shows in some measure how the Party and government keep such close contact with the masses and can so flexibly define policy as the co-op movement takes its swift and complex course.

Old Cottage at Timushan

After a year and more through their own personal experience the peasants had, while seeing the defects, also come to appreciate the advantages of the seasonal mutual-aid teams. With the help of the Party they had searched for and found ways to overcome these defects and so advanced to a higher and better form of co-operation, the seasonal mutual-aid team. Now, with growing understanding of co-operation and how to improve their farming techniques, they grew dissatisfied with the defects of the seasonal mutual-aid team and sought to improve it. Their immediate difficulties were mostly solved. Now they wanted to raise output still higher, to bring more work into planning, to rationalize labour, to still further improve their lives. The seasonal mutual-aid team organization was being outgrown.

Following the autumn harvest of 1951, the Party and peasants summed up the experience of the past year. It was seen that the seasonal mutual-aid team couldn't make long-term, year-round plans for improving production and so couldn't make provision in its plans for the side-occupations of members. And in Hsinteng County, as we have seen, such side-occupations are extremely important to the peasant. Paper-making, for instance, accounted for 40 per cent of some peasants' income. Thus there was a two-way pull on members' loyalties in the seasonal mutual-aid team. At one and the same time there might be a call for collective work, for transplanting seedlings for instance, work which has to be done immediately the seedlings are ready, and on the other, for paper-making, because the pulp has to be used or it will spoil. Then either one or the other job suffered. Many families therefore wanted to have mutual aid in side-occupations as well — that is, form a permanent mutual-aid team which has the advantage of being able to plan all work, both field work and side-occupations.

These pioneer teams worked well throughout the winter of 1951. In Hsu Kuei-yung's team they learnt to plan both field work and side-occupations. This led to more efficient division of labour. Good ploughmen and harrowers specialized in field work, while those who were good at making paper concentrated on this, the hardy ones doing the tough work of washing the paper pulp, the older men and women working at the pulp troughs, or peeling, drying and packing the sheets. Such mutual-aid division of labour applied to paper-making increased output and income. The teams began to accumulate a small amount of commonly-owned property such as barrows, farm tools or draught animals.

Since the scope of planning was increased to the full range of farm labour, suitable work could be found for all members. The women in particular could be drawn more fully into the organization. In the old days, women were debarred by custom from doing field work. Now, as it was possible to find them suitable tasks within their strength, more and more came to the fields. Those who had never done field work before learnt to weed, hoe, collect and put down fertilizer and so on, while those who still specialized in side-occupations like paper-making or silkworm-raising could have their work put into the plan.

All this had a most important effect on their advance to full equality with men. The old rough and ready method of assessing women at "half manpower" and leaving it at that was finally ended. It had been better than no form of assessment at all but soon team members got dissatisfied with it. Some women weren't really even up to "half manpower" and then arguments took place because people were getting from them less than they were paying for. Some women were the equal of men at work, and saw no reason why in New China they should be discriminated against.

The latest method of assessing labour ended all such arguments. By this method, as we shall see, points were fixed to the job rather than the person doing it. This was more like a real system of "equal pay for equal work" based on piece work. Now the team — vastly more experienced in this than a year ago — could assess a particular job very accurately. For instance, weeding a certain wet field might be assessed at five points (half a workday). If the person given the job took more than half a day on it, then he got his five points but lost wages because he could not do another job that day to make up the ten points for a whole workday — unless he pulled up his socks and did better on the second job. If he could do the weeding in less than half a day, that was a clear gain to him. He might then go on to make 12 or more points that day instead of the normal ten. This was a big stimulus to labour, both among the men and women.

With the lesson of such advantages before them in the pioneering permanent mutual-aid teams, more and more of the seasonal mutual-aid teams in the county turned their eyes in this direction. In Chengling District by the late autumn of 1951, 50 per cent of the 450 seasonal mutual-aid teams had turned themselves into permanent, year-round mutual-aid teams.

The advantages of the permanent mutual-aid teams were so obvious that more and more were formed. By the autumn of 1952, a large majority of the peasant households in Chengling District were organized in 279 of these permanent teams with a score or more families in each. Only 17 seasonal teams remained. And the average yield of rice in the district rose to 420 catties a *mou* — an increase of 40 catties over the previous year.

The permanent mutual-aid team has many advantages over the seasonal one, but it, too, has its drawbacks. As time went on team members became increasingly conscious of the irksome difficulties involved. Although labour is exchanged collectively, each individual retains complete control of what is planted on his fields and receives all their produce. So friction inevitably arises between members on some points; the efficiency which collective labour can give is hampered and held back by the selfish demands which individual management of the fields inevitably breeds. As I have already mentioned, the question of whose field should be worked first is always a touchy one in mutual-aid teams, though this conflict may be more or less severe, depending on the amount of team spirit, collective spirit, built up in the team. If seedlings, for instance, are not transplanted just at the proper time, it can mean a heavy loss. During sowing, transplanting and harvest seasons there were not a few disputes about priority and they even led to the break-up of weakly organized teams.

One of the most serious defects of the permanent mutual-aid team, however, is that the amount of labour and fertilizer put into improving a given field is limited by the immediately available resources of its owner. He has to pay for this fertilizer out of his own pocket and must, of course, either pay for or give an equivalent return for the work done on his field. This means that within the team there is a very uneven advance to prosperity. And of course, from the state's point of view, it is difficult to get each smallholder to integrate his little production plan with the over-all district or state plan. It is easy for the peasants to make up their minds to join the permanent mutual-aid team — it does not make too great a demand on their individualism as smallholders — but it is this very feature, inherent in the permanent mutual-aid team form of organization, which prevents it from really bringing into play all the productive possibilities of its members and their land as a whole. Hsu Kuei-yung's mutual-aid team found that as a result of better organized use of labour it had labour to spare and nothing to use it on. Five of the team households had labour to do side-occupations, like making paper, but no capital with which to start work.

As this became clearer to the team members of Hsinteng County they began to look forward to the higher form of co-operation, the agricultural producers' co-operative or farm co-op, which they had heard about in the press, on the radio and at meetings organized by the Party. They heard how the co-op farms had solved just the problems that worried them, and many of them were eager to try out this new method of organization.

Since the mutual-aid teams were in a healthy and flourishing state — the very fact that their members were eager to improve them by trying out better forms of co-op organization showed this — the county leadership felt it wise to encourage the next step forward.

Old county offices in Hsinteng —

CO-OP FARMS

The transformation to the agricultural producers' co-operative involves the pooling of members' land and joint management of all the land so pooled. The Chengling district Party committee knew that this meant a very radical change to the individual small-holding peasants, and so the work of forming co-op farms must be handled with great care. After all-round consultation it was agreed that Hsu Kuei-yung's mutual-aid team, which had been adjudged the best in the county the previous autumn, should be the "key" team for a try-out. The peasants there were keen to go ahead. It was only when, two months later, this team was working smoothly as a co-op farm that the committee helped another seven permanent mutual-aid teams turn themselves into co-ops. That was in the spring of 1952. Chengling District was not behind in the national co-operative movement, considering that in the autumn of 1951, there were only about 400 such co-ops in the whole country.

Experience did indeed show that though the co-op farm is not a fully socialist form of co-operative, it does represent for the peasant a big step forward from the mutual-aid teams. Pooling land as well as labour means voluntarily renouncing the old *laissez-faire* and a great deal of the individualism of the small individual farmer. The co-op member still owns his land and large farm implements and animals, but he voluntarily vests their management and use of his labour in the collective. This is the factor that allows the co-op farm to solve the contradiction that constantly troubled the mutual-aid team — the conflict between joint working of the land and its individual management.

No co-op member, for instance, quarrels about whose land should be ploughed or harvested first. He gets his whole income (except for the produce from his small individual allotment) from the income of the whole farm. In the first year, in most cases about 40 per cent of the net income of the co-op is divided up among members as dividends on their land which they have pooled as shares in the co-op; about five per cent is set aside for welfare and as a capital fund used to buy animals, large tools and other items as common property of the co-op; the rest is divided up among members as remuneration for labour assessed in workdays (with 8 or 10 points usually to the workday). Since each member thus takes his dividend and wages out of the common income pool, it is to his advantage to see that this is as large as possible. The larger the income, the bigger the dividend and the higher the value of workdays. Thus it is to his direct advantage to see that the ploughing or harvesting — and indeed, all work — is done in the most efficient way possible irrespective of whose land it is done on. There is every incentive too to work well no matter whose field one is working on. Even in the permanent mutual-aid team, some backward members worked well on their own land but not nearly so conscientiously on other people's land. When other members noticed this and their land was not affected, they too often said nothing. It wasn't *their* land that suffered and they didn't like to make a fellow member lose face! But in the co-op farm all land is equally the concern of all members. The whole force of public opinion in the co-op is brought to bear on slackers.

These are only some of the main advantages of the co-op over the mutual-aid team. There are many others. The co-op also makes it possible to make more thorough overall plans, to bring more people into the work, to undertake long-term, labour-consuming jobs to improve the land radically, jobs like building dykes, digging ponds, damming rivers and so on. The co-op can use fertilizer more efficiently, organize a better division of labour and use fields more effectively for the crops best suited to them as we shall see in concrete detail when I tell about the Tumushan co-op.

The autumn harvest of 1952 showed the strength of the newly formed co-op farms. Yang Yu-chuan's co-op got an average yield of 483 catties a *mou*, 22 per cent more than the year before. This created quite a sensation. More and more peasants wanted to join co-ops. Ten new co-op farms were formed in quick succession.

But it mustn't be thought that each advance in Hsinteng County was as smooth as butter. Experience has often to be paid for and the county was pioneering new ways of life never before known by China's peasants.

The spectacular success of these first steps in co-operation turned not a few heads on the county committee. Not a few co-ops were set up in a spirit of exuberant enthusiasm that refused to be deterred by such "small" considerations as that some peasants had not quite made up their minds, or quite fully understood the advantages of the co-op.

The more active, go-ahead peasants were eager and proud to be in on the formation of a co-op farm. There was also some idea that a co-op was easier to run than a mutual-aid team. It solved so many tiresome problems at one stroke! Despite warnings from the provincial Party committee against impetuousness and "commandism" (bossiness) and to take care only to advance to the co-op form of organization when the peasants were fully ready for this step, the hotheads continued to press forward.

There was a flurry of reports of successes from the new co-ops. Hsu Kuei-yung's in its eagerness to excel set a target of raising an average yield of 700 catties a *mou* against its nearest rival's 660. This proved to be quite an unreal target as things in the district were then, but for the moment it created a new sensation and added fuel to the flames of enthusiasm.

63

Today, as they talk about that period there are not a few in Hsinteng County who talk ruefully of "getting dizzy with success." The fact was that some of these immature co-ops were poorly organized and many of their members were dissatisfied and confused, so they worked badly and thus tended to discredit the idea of co-operation.

In this heady atmosphere over 100 co-op farms were formed in Chengling District alone within a few months. This was 75 per cent of all the households there, more even than in the plan which the district had proposed the previous June and which the provincial committee had warned was "adventuristic"! The figure for the county was 35 per cent.

Glowing reports from Hsinteng County that gave little hint of any defects naturally brought inquisitive observers down from the provincial Party committee. Cautious, over-cautious eyes refused to be dazzled by the successes they saw. A rapid check showed that many co-ops were in fact paper creations doing more harm than good. Many peasants had voted for them simply out of a feeling that they didn't want to be left out and not out of real conviction that the co-op farm was better than the mutual-aid team. As one said to an official from the rural work department of the provincial Party committee in Hangchow: "I joined, but it wasn't a 'free-choice marriage'!" (Public opinion at that time was very insistent that there should be no more "arranged" marriages in which the partners were not consulted.)

Just at that time too, scandal enveloped Hsu Kuei-yung's co-op farm. By superhuman efforts and uneconomic use of fertilizer, it managed to raise 780 catties a *mou* on a few show-place fields where it had pledged itself to raise 1,000 catties, but the actual average yield was 470 catties a *mou*. This was exceptionally good (70 catties more than the previous year) but far from the promised 700 catties. In a panic, anxious not "to lose face" — Hsu particularly had grown a bit conceited with success: his co-op farm had been constantly in the press and thousands of peasants had come to marvel at it — they reported a false figure, and were promptly found out.

The story was bruited about from end to end of the county, and around the province. It lent vivid colour to the charges of adventurism that were levelled at the county.

Hsu Kuei-yung had let loose more than he knew of. At the first news of the "success" he had been nominated as a "provincial model farmer." It got harder and harder to make a clean breast of the fraud. But once the storm broke he showed the real grit of his character. The only thing to do now was to take the blame and make a full self-criticism. Only this could rehabilitate the co-op and his own character. He did it. The good work he had done before stood him in good stead. But it was an uphill job for a long time to win back the full trust of his fellow members. Most members left the co-op, though they came back later.

However, the evil had been donè. It would have been enough to keep the rush into co-ops under control, to correct the "deviation of bossiness" as it was called, but not only was the rush-forward stopped, it was reversed under the influence of the over-cautious. The charge of adventurism levelled at Hsinteng County by the over-cautious stuck and the authorities refused to register many co-ops. Not too firmly founded, though they might have been consolidated if treated with care, they broke up under this official opposition. In the upshot, the number of households in the co-op farms of Chengling District fell from 75 per cent to only 35 per cent. In the county as a whole the drop was from 35 per cent to 4.5 per cent!

The peasants were told that all who wished were free to withdraw immediately from the new co-ops (normally withdrawals can be made only at the end of the year). The ill-organized co-op farms mostly reverted to their original mutual-aid team status. At the same time, however, a more attentive study of Party policy, frank criticism and self-criticism made a healthier basis than before for a steady advance to co-operation. Over 1,800 activists from the various districts of the county were gathered together at special courses where they could study the situation and the Party's policy and understand what mistakes had been made.

By the end of this episode in the spring of 1953, the 48 co-op farms which had held together, with 4.5 per cent of the households in Hsinteng County, were fully consolidated.

All this left several older and sadder, but wiser heads among the Party workers, officials and activists of Hsinteng County.

This experience was carefully studied not only in the county, but throughout the province. It was publicized in the national press and at conferences on rural work. The successes of Hsinteng County helped to encourage others forward on the road of co-operation. But its mistakes too were made to serve a useful purpose — to prevent similar mistakes from being made elsewhere. It was a serious lesson to all that every advance in the co-op movement must be carefully prepared.

That winter of 1953, with a better understanding of things, the peasants summed up the year's work. They, like everyone else in the nation, studied the General Line of the Communist Party for the advance of the country to socialism and, with the example of the good co-op farms in front of them, there was a fresh wave of enthusiasm for co-operation. To advance to socialism — to industrialization, to new, secure strength for the nation, to prosperity— means that the little individual farms must be united into stronger economic units able to use modern farming methods with mechanized equipment on a large scale, and able to take a reliable part in over-all state plans. The forward-looking peasants of Hsinteng County could see this meant, in the first place, the organization of strong co-op farms.

The movement advanced steadily throughout that winter of 1953, and by the end of 1954 some 70 per cent of all households in the county were in co-op farms, with most of the rest in permanent mutual-aid teams. In Chengling District the figure was 88 per cent.

The advance to the co-op farms brought to a head the problem of relations with the old type of rich peasant.

The aim of the co-op movement is to make all peasants rich, but the question of the rich peasant left over from the old days is quite another matter.

Land reform finished the Hsinteng landlords as a class but the farms of the rich peasants were not touched unless they had been guilty of exceptionally oppressive practices in renting out surplus land under feudal conditions. Old rich peasants formed three per cent of the population of the county, but they owned nearly five per cent of the land even after the land reform.

In addition to their economic influence, which was not negligible, they were also a source of backward ideas and ways among the peasants.

It should not be thought that the rich peasant was necessarily a good farmer. He was usually merely cunning in exploiting his labourers, robbing poor peasants by making loans at exorbitant interest and speculating in farm produce. These were perfectly normal practices under the Kuomintang regime, but in New China there is no place for them. Wanting to retain and increase their wealth, they naturally looked to the old ways of doing it. Those were the only ways that, up to the liberation, the peasants of Hsinteng had ever heard of for getting rich. So it was natural that if mutual aid started on the morrow of the land reform so too did its opposite — the spontaneous tendency to differentiation among the peasants into rich and poor along capitalist lines, with the small grasping minority trying to push themselves forward to relative prosperity at the expense of their fellows. A decisive conflict between these two ways of life was inevitable — co-operation v. exploitation; socialism v. capitalism.

Since the spring of 1953 and 1954, the period when the county was making the biggest advances in the co-op movement, the rich peasants had, in fact, been finding it increasingly difficult to hold their own. It was difficult to hire labourers to exploit; all the peasants had their own land to look after now and had their mutual-aid teams and co-ops in which they could use their labour profitably enough. Credit co-ops too were putting an end to high-interest loans and usury. The supply and marketing co-ops and the system of state buying and supply of grain and other staple agricultural products had in the main put an end to speculation.

All this and the Communist Party's programme for the general advance to socialism put great and increasing restrictions on the rich peasants' activities. Some rich peasants were forced to accept what they could see was the inevitable; these sought to come to peaceful terms with the new society by conscientiously obeying the laws and reforming themselves so that they could be accepted into the new social and economic organizations of the peasants. But the die-hards among the rich peasants stubbornly resisted the changes in the countryside and actively sabotaged and tried to discredit the co-op movement, which was making their selfish way of life impossible.

They wormed their way into mutual-aid teams and co-op farms where they feathered their own nests and stirred up trouble from within. They used their ability to read and keep accounts to get into key positions. Taking advantage of the still considerable peasant illiteracy, they cooked accounts to cause dissatisfaction among members, and set one group against another. They tried blackmail and bribery to corrupt co-op members. When Chen Ah-go, a rich peasant of Tungpu Township, found a number of peasants in Chen Ho-tai's mutual-aid team in financial difficulties due to a poor crop, with a great show of benevolence he hired 14 of them to work for him ... and the team broke up.

In Yungho Township Wu Ah-yin, a rich peasant, got her widowed daughter-in-law to ensnare members so that they neglected their work in the mutual-aid team; she offered high wages to attract members to work for her rather than for the team and finally succeeded in disintegrating it.

Ho Pei-yen married off his two buxom daughters to leaders of two mutual-aid teams, tricked his sons-in-law and several other team members into working for him, and thus for a time discredited the very idea of forming mutual-aid teams in the neighbourhood. Other rich peasants got into teams as tallymen by "generously" offering to lend animals or tools and then, diddling the members, discredited the teams. Through their big clan family connections some even formed false teams or co-ops, then used these to buy goods from the supply and marketing co-ops and speculate with them.

Some rich peasant tricks were as ingenious as they were stupid. One rich peasant gave extra doses of fertilizer to plants in a field bordering that of a co-op just to crow over the bumper harvest private enterprise could reap when compared to collective farming!

Why did the peasants let the rich peasants join their teams and co-op farms? It must be remembered that these districts were pioneering entirely new paths for China and some very confused ideas about the rich peasants were current at the outset of the movement. Some said that "the rich peasants have a vote like any other honest farmer, so why shouldn't they be allowed to join?" Some said that "if the rich peasants were discriminated against, that would discourage other peasants from raising production to get rich." Some said that "rich peasants have big houses — they're useful for meetings; they are educated and can do accounting while most of the poor peasants are still illiterate; they have money to lend to members in need;

and they have animals and tools which can also be used to help the team or co-op." Naturally this "theory" of the "four benefits from rich peasants" was assiduously spread by them and their hangers-on. Short-sighted people failed to see what lay behind all these "advantages" of admitting rich peasants.

There were also quite a few team leaders who found it especially easy to get along with the rich peasants when they joined the teams. These people were so polite, no haggling or back answers from them! Besides, they urged, there weren't many of them, so what harm could they do? So ran the facile arguments of complacency.

Other rich peasants tried to disorganize the unified state purchase and sale of grain. One Ma Chi-shui of Chengling District hid nearly 1,000 catties of grain, some of it in his coffin, and then went to the state trading agency demanding to buy grain because he was "threatened with starvation." He was exposed when an observant co-op member noticed the weight of the supposedly empty coffin.

Anti-co-op elements didn't hesitate to commit acts of flagrant sabotage. In Chengling District, they burnt down the stables and killed livestock belonging to the Chung Ying-feng Co-op, led by a woman chairman.

But such rich peasants underrated the new spirit in the countryside. One by one their subterfuges were found out and unmasked. Armed with the facts, the Party was able to show the peasants what the activities of the rich peasants were leading to. In the upshot, the peasants of the county saw to it that only those rich peasants — some 10 per cent of the total — who had good records in the past, had given up exploitation and proved to be law-abiding, were allowed into the teams and co-op farms after each case was thoroughly discussed by members. They had learnt that "to keep a rich peasant in your team is like feeding a tiger in your stable!" They understood better the wisdom of the Party directive that in developing the co-operative move-

71

ment basic reliance must be placed on the poor peasants working in alliance with the middle peasants, and that today, as the country advances to socialism, the policy must be to restrict the rich-peasant economy and gradually eliminate it as incompatible with socialism. The rich peasants are the last remaining exploiting class in the countryside.

All the other rich peasants were told that if they resolutely gave up their malpractices and behaved themselves properly, they would in the future be allowed to join co-ops provided these were well and strongly organized and the members agreed.

Later, in a township where the peasants had formed a big collective farm with over 90 per cent of the population in it, I saw how this problem was disposed of in actual fact. Here rich peasants, who had been kept in political and economic check as the co-op movement had got into its stride, were finally admitted to the collective farm. They were few in number, their economic and political influence was now negligible. As a matter of fact they were eager to pool their land and other means of production and glad to be rid of the taint of the old "rich-peasant status." The collective farm yields were already surpassing the yields they could get as individual rich peasants. As one farm committee member said: "They'll complete their socialist remoulding inside the collective farm."

The successes of the co-op movement in the county and the setbacks it suffered at the hands of the rich peasants again underlined for the peasants the wisdom of the Party directive: "Rely on the poor peasants, unite with the middle peasants, isolate and restrict the rich peasants and gradually abolish them as a class!"

A similarly humane policy was being followed for those landlords and their families who did not oppose or sabotage the people's laws. After the land reform they were given land like other peasants. If they had not been guilty of criminal activities, but only of normal landlord exploitation, they were allowed to reform themselves through labour under general surveillance. The peasants charged with their surveillance keep an eye on them to see they don't get up to any counter-revolutionary activities. If they get into financial difficulties this is also reported to the people's authorities and help is given them. If their records are good, five years after the land reform such landlords will receive back their civil rights.

Theatre at Chengling —

HIGHER YIELDS, A BETTER LIFE

By 1955 the more efficient organization of labour and use of fields enabled the co-ops to increase yields steadily year by year. They already surpassed those of the most efficient of the old landlord and rich-peasant farms of the past.

In 1954 the county's average yield was 400 catties of grain a *mou* and the total output 41,500,000 catties, an increase of about one-third since liberation. (Bad weather had reduced the yield from 422 catties a *mou* in 1953.)

With higher yields the villagers were living better than they ever did before. Some 70 per cent of co-op members were new middle peasants. Average annual incomes in the co-ops ranged around 1,200 catties of grain per person. (A grown man needs about 500 catties of rice a year for food.) Compare this with the 460 catties that Pien Chu-shen, chairman of the Chingho Collective Farm, got before the land reform and the 1,100 he got in 1953.

The hamlets were clean. New houses were going up. No longer did you see ragged peasants on the roads. They wore neat cotton-padded suits in winter, galoshes and raincoats when it rained. Their woollen sweaters, fountain-pens, torchlights, a quilt for every person — these were undreamt-of luxuries five years ago. Now they excited no special comment. Better living had wiped out the gambling, drinking and petty thievery that were a curse of the district under the Kuomintang. Relaxation of economic worries led to happier family life.

The peasants were also making a constantly increasing contribution to the national well-being. Partly by reclaiming waste land, but mainly by increasing yields, Chengling District increased its output of rice from 7,640,000 catties in 1949, with an average yield of 300 catties a *mou*, to 10,340,000 catties in 1954 with an average yield of 406 catties a *mou*. And in addition it produced increasing amounts of the industrial crops the country needs. The output of vegetable oil in the county as a whole increased from 1,000,000 to 1,600,000 catties. The output of tea, silk, paper, bamboo and other products also rose.

But the Hsinteng peasants were far from being complacent about such achievements. They knew very well that the road they were travelling could lead to far greater heights of prosperity for themselves and their country.

In 1955, on the basis of improvements to the soil already made, they planned to introduce a completely new system of cultivation. By planting two crops of rice, either following one another in quick succession or planting "between the rows," or by planting a single, late-ripening, high-yielding variety, they would get yields of between 500 and 550 catties a *mou*. They cleared and improved more land, planted orchards, bamboo groves, tea gardens, maize and other new and more valuable crops and also raised more livestock and poultry. These would bring a further sharp rise in incomes.

From being one of the poorest areas in Chekiang, they aimed at catching up with such places as Linghai where yields of 600 to 700 catties of rice a *mou* are the rule.

With prosperity growing throughout the country, the people's government was also able to give greater assistance to the movement in Hsinteng County, both financial and technical. In 1953, the People's Bank extended loans of various kinds amounting to 186,600 yuan, which was 138,400 yuan more than the previous year. By 1954, the bank was supplemented by a flourishing credit co-op movement. Together they loaned the peasants 234,000 yuan, mostly to expand production. Requests for loans because of "family difficulties" have steadily decreased.

In 1953 a state farm and a farming instructional centre were set up to popularize better scientific methods. In 1954 a training class was started for co-op accountants.

Although the semi-socialist co-op farm was still regarded in official plans as the main form of co-operation for the moment, some of the peasants in Hsinteng County were already looking to get still higher yields by still more advanced methods of co-operative organization. Last summer, they formed four collective farms in the county, one of which, Pien Chu-shen's, was in Chengling District. In these fully socialist collective farms, members abolished dividends on land shares. The bulk of the farm's income, after setting aside sums for current expenditure, welfare and long-term investments, went for payment for labour on the socialist principle, "to each according to his work." This ended the contradiction between private landownership and collective labour, and opened the way to develop all the great possibilities of the peasants working as a brotherly collective on unencumbered, jointly managed fields.

The greater reserves of the collective farm enable it to provide adequate insurance benefits to members. Its higher income gives members bigger incomes from labour alone than they got in the co-op farm from land-share dividends and wages combined. It is worth while pointing out here that the increased grain output has been achieved almost entirely with the old tools or only some few improved tools. There is none of the mechanization that will be available when, in the near future, China is able to produce the tractors and other machinery needed for large-scale mechanized agriculture. Mechanization will open up even bigger possibilities of increased production.

By the spring of 1955, co-operation had become the rule of the economic and social life of Hsinteng County. Over 75 per cent of all the peasant households in the county were in co-op farms. Most of the rest were in mutual-aid teams.* In Chengling District the figures were even higher: 88 per cent of the households were in co-op farms, and even the few remaining individual peasants were embraced by the "networks" of mutual aid that are grouped around the leading co-ops of the various localities.

All key productive activities of the county were linked with state plans through the unified state purchase and supply of grain and other main products. The growth of consumers', handicraft and credit co-ops severed the old links with middlemen and commercial capitalist exploitation and usury.

The Hsinteng peasants had emerged on to the broad co-operative road to prosperity.

---

*In Chekiang Province as a whole some 30 per cent of the peasant households were in mutual-aid teams and another 30 per cent in co-op farms. In China as a whole 14 per cent of the peasant households had joined co-op farms at this time.

SMALL INTERLUDE: TRAVELLERS' TALES

It was a cold February afternoon in 1955.

We brought our packs and baggage out to load on to the rubber-tired wheelbarrow of the type that is used for light cartage on the narrow, hilly tracks of Chengling District. The whole thing weighed about 500 lbs., but the long-limbed young carrier handled it with ease. He expeditiously stowed the bedding, typewriter and bags so that they balanced evenly over the wheel, took up the handles and, with a jaunty air, set off at a fast pace. He was used to making twenty or thirty *li* trips with 1,000 lb. loads, and now we had only a five *li* trip to do on a good, flat highway. He gossiped gaily on the way.

"There's a cave about fifteen *li* from here, so big that a thousand people can shelter in it. Countless birds nest there and every year a hundred peasants go there to collect their nests and droppings for fertilizer!"

This was all said with a tone of absolute, circumstantial assurance. When we had commented suitably on it and asked further questions which he answered with equal assurance, he continued:

"About fifty *li* from here there's another cave. That's a real wonder! I went there to see it myself. You let yourself down a hole in the ground like a well. In its side you see an opening. Very narrow. Just big enough for a man to squeeze through. Then it suddenly broadens out into a huge room as big as a meeting hall. There are stone tables there and stools, stone drums and bugles. The local people say that it used to be a fairy hall, but that only ghosts go there now!"

We all commented in some surprise at this, eagerly asking the exact location of this wonder and speculating on its scientific significance and archaeological value. Perhaps it was a home of neolithic man? Or the meeting place of some forgotten secret society?

"About seventy-five *li* from here there is a spring which gushes every now and again out of a hole in a rock. Sweet, clear water. It forms a stream and in the first two hundred feet of that stream there breeds a special kind of cockle.

"The Emperor Chien Lung once went there especially to eat those cockles. They have no stomachs and so their insides are perfectly clean. There are no other cockles like this anywhere else around here!" And he added, as if in an afterthought, "Or anywhere else in the world!"

These stories interspersed with descriptions of the countryside and farmsteads we were passing, fleeting conversations with everyone else we encountered on the road, conversations which lasted a good hundred feet from start to finish—brought us at length to the Chengling district centre.

It was already dark. The young carrier mopped his close-cropped head with the towel he wore round his neck. He darted inside the district office where a bright light burnt, and a minute or so after reappeared with the receipt he had written out for his carrier fee. He belonged to one of the Wang Wen-ken Co-op teams which was doing this work as a winter side line.

Then he wished us an abrupt but cheery good-bye and disappeared into the twilight.

We half wondered whether this lively young co-op farmer really believed in ghosts and fairies.

"Why does he tell us these tales?" we asked the young county official who had accompanied us. This was a silent young man who had spoken little on the walk. Now he thought for a moment and then replied with great finality:

"Why, these are strange tales for strange people!"
We're still wondering. . . .

III

CO-OP FARM AT TUMUSHAN

The following is the story of the co-operative movement in the village of Tumushan, in Hsinteng County of Chekiang Province, just as the peasants there told it to me sometimes in their homes, a simple cottage, or in the former mansion of a landlord, sometimes on the verge of their fields as they rested from work. I have tried to keep the story substantially as they told it. The accuracy with which they remembered events long since past, figures of yields and methods of work was astonishing. If there are any inadequacies in this report it is entirely due to my clumsiness in taking down their unaffected, lively descriptions.

It would take a much more skilled recorder than myself to convey the deep human warmth of their words and the courage and resilience of spirit with which they battled their way through incredible difficulties and are now, under the leadership of the Communist Party, making their way to a life of socialist prosperity.

RAGS TO RICHES

It was the summer of 1949. The wheat was yellow and ripe for harvesting. The rice seedlings were ready for transplanting, but the peasants of Tumushan had gathered, every one of them, outside the ancestral hall in the hamlet, to hear a speech by the new people's government official.

None of them knew him. Broad faced, thick set, standing there strong as a rock, a man in a faded yellow uniform, they could see he was a Northerner. He wore a holster with a wide leather strap slung over his shoulder. In it was a revolver carefully wrapped in red silk.

The old Kuomintang village head stood there by him looking very uncomfortable.

The villagers didn't clearly know what this new government stood for. A few days before, the Kuomintang troops had taken themselves off — and good riddance —

after exchanging a few shots with a detachment of peasant fighters who had long been battling them from up in the hills. "Bandits" the landlords called them, but the peasants knew them as bolder, perhaps more desperate than most, but peasants nevertheless, like themselves. Then an army with red banners passed through the valley chasing the Kuomintangites. They left a few men in Hsinteng county town and a few in the big village down the main road. It was one of these who had asked the Tumushan people to come to a meeting.

The bolder ones stood quite close to hear him. The timid ones hung around on the edges by the bamboos trying to catch what he said, but pretending not to be listening too closely. The Kuomintang garrison had gone but Landlord Hu was still a power. Snooper Wang, who tattled to him, was there at the meeting, and there were still a lot of Kuomintang troops and landlords' *pao an tuan* — peace preservation corps(!) — up in the hills. And only those five new officials in the village up the road.

"Where are you from?" someone called out.

"From Shantung," he answered, "from Chairman Mao Tse-tung." The name struck a chord. That was the leader of the Communist Party!

Then he gave a speech.

The truth is the villagers didn't understand much of what he said. It was about a people's army and a people's government — but the Kuomintang had talked that way once and it hadn't meant a thing! Then he said they'd get peace and land. That sounded good. But then they remembered that Landlord Hu was listening. He'd said the Kuomintang would be sure to come back!

Then there was a lot about "rice dumplings."* "Rice dumplings" this and "rice dumplings" that! It was all very puzzling.

---

*The Shantung pronunciation of *nung min*, "peasants," sounds like the Chekiang *no mi*, "rice for dumplings."

But there was one thing different about this official that they all understood. He was a working man like one of them. They could see that from his hands. Hands that could hold a hammer or a hoe or a rifle.

But the puzzlement didn't last long. Hsinteng County didn't have telephones or radio as it does now, but the news quickly got around. Those new Shantung peasant officials lived with the poorest of peasants and hired labourers and told them more about the people's government. The villagers soon got to understand their talk, and they, the local dialect. When they said they were from the same army as the New Fourth Army,* that made things clearer. The New Fourth Army had been in these parts some years back, in 1945. The Kuomintang had attacked them but they had chased the Kuomintang troops back and had come to several villages hereabouts. Those soldiers had been very good to the peasants, helping them in every way. When they wanted to buy vegetables they always told the young people to consult with their elders, before fixing a price! Still one had to think of one's family. The older ones among the peasants hung back. There were too many unfriendly eyes around. But the young people got bolder and bolder.

It wasn't long before a score or more of Tumushan lads were in the people's militia which was formed. They carried rifles and shotguns, some of them a bit ancient. There was Wang Wen-ken, one of the first to join, he's the vice-chairman of the co-op now and one of the two local Party members, the present township Party branch secretary was another, and Wang Kuan-lin too, he's the Tumushan co-op accountant now. The rest were also all young chaps, and all working well now in the co-op movement or the people's government or Communist Party.

---

*During the war against the Japanese invaders, the Eighth Route Army and the New Fourth Army were led by the Communist Party.

The reactionaries were doing all they could to harass the new government: spreading rumours, sometimes shooting. Once in August they came down to raid one of the districts. They surrounded the house where the comrades from Shantung had their office and tried to shoot them up. But they escaped. The raiders were afraid to burn down the house and catch them that way because it belonged to a landlord. The next time they came the people were ready for them: they were met with bullets.

That September, when the rice fields were golden yellow, a detachment of the people's army came back from the front to the county. This time the Tumushan peasants went down the road to meet them with flags. They killed a pig and roasted it to welcome them. The detachment had come to help mop up the Kuomintang bandits and the young people went with them. The bandits were a poor lot, just like the Kuomintang army. Some were killed, some surrendered and the rest slipped back to where they came from. That was the end of them. But for Tumushan it was the real beginning of life.

But now you must know something about this village of Tumushan — Top of the Tu Family Grave Mountain. Nestling in the hollow between two hills that jut out into the wide valley of the Sung Creek, it is a typically picturesque little hamlet in Chengling District. The dozen or so peasant homes all cling to one side of the hollow, overlooking the fields which rise in terraces, the highest some thirty feet above the valley floor. A stream falls in a series of small cascades from terrace to terrace, nourishing the fields and providing an ample supply of water for the chief side-occupation of the peasants — paper-making. Around a pool at the back of the village stands a ring of nine bamboo and straw sheds, each sheltering a paper-making trough.

Like everywhere else in China, in Tumushan there is the contrast between old and new. There are old thatched cottages with adobe and wattle walls (the worst have been turned into stalls for animals now) and sturdy old homes built a century ago of stone and fine timber. They were built crowded together to save precious land. But among them stands a newly whitewashed and repaired house and the rising walls of two new homes built with large and airy rooms. They all belong to former poor peasants, now co-operative farmers of today. At the entrance to the hamlet stands the old ancestral temple. Among the houses is a club-room with a radio.

Nearly everyone in Tumushan is surnamed Wang. The Wang clan traces its descent through twenty generations from a former high official, and the tablets in the ancestral temple and clan register are there to prove it. It must have been a wealthy clan. An inscription over one of the ancestral halls reads: "Exalted Family of the State of Yueh" as this part of Chekiang was once called. Then the Wangs were scattered through a dozen villages: Wangs rich and poor, landlords and landless labourers. Clan solidarity was still centred around the ancestral temples where the clan heads gathered on solemn occasions. Mostly it would be to administer punishment to one of its poorer members. The Wang rich, grinding the very life out of the Wang poor and any others who fell into their net of rent and usury, used the appeal of clan solidarity to prevent revolt against their power to exploit.

It was the Wang rich and landlords who controlled clan affairs. It was they who supervised the ancestral lands which belonged in theory to the whole clan and which were cultivated in turn by the landless members of the clan, preserving them from the utter destitution that constantly threatened completely landless labourers.

The Wang rich and other landlords were not perhaps very rich by modern standards of monopoly wealth, but they lived in fine houses with expensive carvings on their columns, and paintings on their walls. They owned scores or even hundreds of *mou* of land where a peasant would consider himself lucky if he owned half a dozen. They dressed well and warmly. They spent as much on a single feast as a poor peasant family would spend in a month of Sundays. And they did this by the most ruthless exploitation of the people. They demanded and got anything from 50 to 80 per cent of the yield of the land they rented out. Over 300 per cent a year interest on a short-term loan was nothing unusual; 100 per cent interest per annum on a loan was an everyday affair. Wang Wen-ken's family paid 170 catties in rent out of each 240 catties of rice they raised per *mou*. After buying fertilizer and renting a buffalo to plough, the peasants sometimes had only the rice straw left for themselves to make paper with. And with all this went the usual tyranny of beatings and killings, kidnapping and pressganging for the Kuomintang government, forced labour and petty squeeze. They used the crudest forms of exploitation. Their farming was inefficient. Their heavy landlord yoke prevented the peasants from ever rising out of the slough of debt so that they could till their fields in peace and raise good crops and wealth for themselves and the country. The feudal yoke of the landlords kept the peasants and the country poor and weak.

By contrast, the Wang and other poor were the poorest of the poor by any standards. Wang Wen-ken, Wang Pao-yuan, Wang Tse-liang, Wang Yuen-liang, and scores of others, all had the same story to tell; a story of rags, cold and starvation. At liberation all the Wangs of Tumushan were poor peasants, all but one — Wang Hsueh-nan.

Wang Wen-ken's keen eyes clouded as he told of the past. He's young. Just 28 years old. His broad forehead is clear. His mouth seems ever ready to smile, but he is serious as he thinks of the old days. He presses home the points he wants to stress with long fingers like a musician's, drumming on the table top.

"We had practically no land of our own — just half a *mou*. We got our turn every four years to till the ancestral land, but that was poor help anyway. When your turn came to till it, you had to pay the land tax on it and arrange a big feast in honour of the ancestors. Twenty-two households had to be invited to that feast — and everyone either hungry or greedy! If you got 60 catties of rice from that land you had to pay 16 as land tax and after the feast there'd not be much left. And your share of land changed every few years. Sometimes it would be 10 *mou*, sometimes only two. And it got worse and worse as time went on because nobody was interested in putting in fertilizer to improve it. You couldn't refuse your turn but you could mortgage it, and we were usually so hard pressed we usually did so a year ahead to some rich peasant who'd give us 300 catties for a share worth over 1,000 to him. And you'd still have to give the feast.

"We had four in the family: my mother, my wife and father. We men could both work full time. ('Father' was really my uncle. My own family had asked him to adopt me because there was me and my brother — two able-bodied young men in my own family and one of us would be sure to be pressganged if we remained together.) We rented six *mou* of land and paid over 40 catties as rent out of every 60 catties we raised. That left us with food for about two months in the year. When that was done we'd borrow from a merchant to buy straw and lime for making rough toilet paper. A block of paper, over a thousand sheets, I remember, was worth about 1.30 yuan (in our money today) but the merchant would give us only 90 cents for it, and call the rest interest on the loan. Then we'd try to borrow from the landlord and he'd take 50 to 100 per cent on that loan. When everything ran out we'd do like everyone else here and live on grass and grass roots in the winter, and whatever other scraps we could find. Cold and hunger never left us in winter. And I was lucky. I had a padded jacket — I'd had only two all my life before liberation. There was only one quilt for the three of us. In summer we went barefoot, in winter we wrapped our feet in straw and scraps of cloth. And there were people here worse off than we were!

"That was the kind of life we were freed from by the People's Liberation Army!

"So now you can see why it was that as soon as we got to understand things a bit we young people joined up with the revolutionary workers. That was when they started the movement against local despots and to lower rents and interest rates.

"That Comrade Chin who had come to us first and the others taught us how to understand who were our real enemies. We learnt how to distinguish the hired labourers and poor peasants and the middle peasants from the landlords and rich peasants whether they called themselves Wang or not. If the peasants were to be freed, get land and build a prosperous life then the landlords had to be overthrown, they said. Well, we began with the worst of them — Landlord Hu.

"That was a regular tyrant! He had been *pao* head for so long that he'd got the nickname 'Old *Pao* Head.' It was he who organized the pressganging of the young men. He used the threat of it to blackmail the peasants. He was always being feasted and the young people worked for him free as short term labourers just to get on the right side of him. Even when the people came to a meeting to make complaints against him they were afraid to talk. It was only when we tied his hands and stood him there helpless before them that they cried out their accusations. There wasn't much in the way of landlord crimes that he wasn't guilty of. He was handed over to the courts and his land confiscated. It was shared out among the most needy families that he'd exploited in the past.

"We remembered what the revolutionary comrades had said when they first came. 'We Communists stand for the peasants. You'll get peace and land! Happiness lies ahead!' Now it was coming true.

"I'd come gradually to know something about the Communist Party policies by that time. I'd joined the people's militia. Wang Chih-shou, who's our township Party branch secretary, and Wang Kuan-lin, who's our co-op accountant, we all joined. I was elected head of our village militia. We went out on patrol against the Kuomintang bandits and arrested other despots. I helped to get the mass organizations started in the village: the peasants' association, Youth League and so on. I was appointed head of this hamlet. I was also accepted into the Party.

"That was a busy time. I worked with the work team which was in charge of the land reform. Every campaign brought more and more of us peasants here into action, and by the end of the land reform there were few of the 23 families here who weren't organized in one movement or the other."

The land reform took place here in Szeho Township in the summer of 1950, a bit earlier than in most other places in the county.

We were talking about it one evening in Wang Hsueh-yung's place after a supper of rice, and four bowls of pickled vegetables, salted turnips, bean-curd fermented till it tastes like good Gorgonzola, and salted fish.

Wang Hsueh-yung has a young, somewhat bony and serious face like his brother Wang Wen-ken. He seems to take a serious view of life while his wife, Ho Hsi-erh, is just the opposite, full of laughter and jokes that make even him suddenly blossom out with a smile that almost becomes a laugh. She has rosy cheeks glowing with health and thick braids of glossy black hair. She is a buxom young woman who can lift baskets of grain of a weight that can make many a man stagger.

Wang Hsueh-yung answered my question: "You wonder how we tilled the land before liberation? Well, now we look back we sometimes wonder too! Some of us didn't even have proper tools. We'd have to borrow them from friends. The landlords and rich peasants wouldn't rent out their buffaloes by the day, so one of us would have to rent on a long term basis, putting up a hefty deposit and then rent it out short term. In the busy seasons it was a regular scramble. Sometimes we'd harrow by harnessing a man to a ladder and use that!

"Land reform put paid to the landlords. They've never worried us since. And it put us all on our feet."

"We had only half a *mou* of land before. Now we've got sixteen," put in his wife. "We got a share of a buffalo too. But the landlord had nearly worn it out. It nearly died on us!" she joked.

Friends had drifted in and joined animatedly in the talk, eager to recall those happy days. The women sat in the outer light peeling apart the dry sheets of paper, ready for packing. The light of the oil lamp flickered over their smiling faces and the warm brown of the beams overhead.

"Wang Wen-ken also only had half a *mou* before. Now he's got 13 for the five in his family," someone interjected.

"I got 11 *mou* for my family of five. Good soil!" announced Wang Tse-liang, a former poor peasant, eager to take part in the conversation.

"And a water-wheel!" someone added.

"Wang Pao-yuan, what did you get?" asked Hsueh-yung, although everyone there knew the answer.

Pao-yuan, a sturdy old peasant, full of energy and interest in all that's going on, almost shouts the answer: "Six *mou* for my family of three!"

Ho Hsi-erh brought in two big bowls of *yu to* which taste like Jerusalem artichokes, and we all set to with a will, talking the while.

"When in 1950 we finally got the land that we had dreamt about all our lives, some of us thought that that was already heaven on earth. Well it was, compared to the past.

"But the land wasn't everything. There just weren't enough farm tools to go round. Of the 23 households here only three had buffaloes. Only three had big water-wheels. Not one household could work independently without difficulty. Some had plenty of labour power, grown-up people — men of the family, but most hadn't enough. We all needed outside help of some kind. You see, transplanting seedlings, for instance, must all be done in one or two days; but an able-bodied man at most can transplant two *mou* a day. Not all here can plough, or harrow well either. So we formed a work-exchange team."

"In the past, we'd naturally helped each other," continued Wang Hsueh-yung, "but this was different. Comrade Chin who was working in this district knew about the work-exchange teams that had been organized in Shantung during the war against the Japanese invaders and in the Liberation War. He helped us organize one here."

The Tumushan peasants chuckled as they talked about this team. Compared to their big, well-run co-op of sixty-two households it was such a primitive thing!

"Work exchange was only organized during the busy seasons on a job to job basis. 'You help harvest my field and I'll help you on yours.' But we hadn't learnt real team work as yet. We used to haggle over what was a fair exchange, since we didn't have any good method of assessing work done. All men were rated alike. Most often as not too many people came to do a particular job. There was waste of manpower and time; too much gossiping and smoking.

"Feudal ideas were still strong. Women didn't work in the fields. People thought it was shameful for them to show any bare flesh but their face and hands. So even the poorest wore some sort of stockings. They could only work around the house and sort and dry paper. They didn't dare take off their slippers to work in the wet fields.

"Still those work-exchange teams brought us benefits. They were a big help to those peasant families who had little able-bodied manpower like Tsao Tsai-erh. Her husband had been pressganged by the KMT and then had gone over to the PLA as soon as he got the chance. He hadn't come back yet.

"We had 35 strong men in our hamlet. All pulling together we could take care of the 190 *mou* we owned. We could all use the water-wheels and the few animals we had by paying their owners a reasonable rental. In the old days only relatives and close friends co-operated like that. We didn't have to give meals as we did in the old times to those who helped us. That was a big relief.

"And remember, the bumper harvest of 1950 was our first crop on our own land. We poor peasants really felt united. We got 315 catties of unhusked rice a *mou* on an average compared to the 240 or so before liberation."

"Although that was only a temporary effort, we got a lasting lesson from it: unity is strength!" summed up Wang Wen-ken. "The peasants were well satisfied with its results despite its troubles. That was important, because it was a foundation for all that came later, though at that time none of us really knew where we were heading."

Wang Wen-ken continued the tale:

"We'd got such good results from the work-exchange team that when the time came for spring work in 1951, we naturally thought about reviving it. But this time we were wiser. The Party organizations and peasants' associations in the district and county had been studying how the

93

various groups and teams in the area had worked. We passed on and exchanged experiences at meetings for exchanging ideas. The press too was full of news about seasonal
mutual-aid teams. And finally it was decided that it was
better to organize smaller, more easily run seasonal mutual-

Mulberry Grove In Winter

aid teams (seasonal MATs), that membership must be
absolutely voluntary and benefits really mutual.

"We formed two temporary teams in our hamlet. One
was led by Chu Cheng-teh with 14 households. I was
elected to lead the other with eight. Many people had
clearly seen from experience what were the weak points
of the work-exchange team, so it wasn't difficult to persuade
them to try out new methods which the seasonal mutual-
aid teams were using. Hsinyen Village is quite close by

and the seasonal team there led by Hsu Kuei-yung was one of the best in the district at that time.

"We found things went much better in the seasonal MAT. We could organize work more efficiently. As team leader I distributed work among our eight households. This cut down waste of manpower. Then we learnt a better way of assessing labour from Hsu Kuei-yung's team. Everyone in the team was assessed a certain number of points according to his capacity and skill, but the actual number of points earned was only finally settled when the job was finished and had been inspected. Then he might get the full number of points or less as the case might be. We used to meet every evening to discuss how many points each should get. This method of assessment was called 'fixed points applied flexibly,' but we weren't too clever about the flexible application part. We were still not too well knit as a team so we usually only criticized members about whether they were late on the job, we didn't like to make people ashamed by criticizing the quality of their work. Still this method did encourage members to do their work better because now they were surer of getting full value for their work. It was a big improvement over the rough 'half-manpower,' 'whole-manpower' system of assessment we used before. We used to call that method 'stomach accounting' — you only complained if it hurt you really bad. Otherwise you just grumbled. No one was really satisfied with it.

"The new method also gave a fair chance for the women to come into the field work. Women didn't work in the work-exchange team partly because there was no good method of assessing the work they did, no man wanted to exchange work with a woman.

"Now since work was assessed by points it was possible to balance a woman's work against a man's. Ideas about women had also changed. Ho Hsi-erh, Wang Hsueh-yung's wife, was the first to come out to work in the fields. The old stick-in-the-muds thought her completely shameless! But she could work as well as many a man. Tsao Tsai-erh was next. The backward elements didn't dare criticize her to her face. Her husband was a volunteer fighting for the country in Korea and she was working 'to support the front!'

"Once the women got a lead they joined in the work one after another. This was a big gain in manpower for our teams. The women do some work better than men."

And it opened a new life for the women. It meant real economic equality, real emancipation.

Members of this type of team worked better than they had in the past. This, plus the better organization of collective work, and more manpower, gave good results. Thus Wang Wen-ken's seasonal mutual-aid team raised 380 catties a *mou* compared to the 315 catties of the old work-exchange team of the year before.

Wang Wen-ken had spoken about the successes of the team with animation. But it was a sober, carefully balanced account. He gave many examples of the various little gains that co-operative work had brought about — better team spirit, mutual emulation, that had led to better sowing, better weeding, better cultivation and harvesting. That extra yield they got was the fruit of something that was difficult to measure. It was a new content — the germ of socialist co-operation — that had entered into the life and work of the peasants of Tumushan, and would grow in strength steadily year by year.

"The winter of 1951, like that of 1950, was taken up with discussions on the work of the past year." Wang Wen-ken continued. "I went to a special study course for Party members in the county town, as I had been admitted to the Party in the early days of land reform. There were 200 of us in the county by this time. I got a better idea what socialism and the Party policy is. I understood then better why we must form mutual-aid teams and then organize co-operatives in order to advance to socialism. But the practical details of how to run a MAT, how to make it work really well — this was the urgent question. So we paid particular attention to reports from comrades who had already formed them in the county. Later on we got the Party decisions on mutual aid and co-operation.* Then things were clearer yet.

"When I came back to Tumushan everyone was eager to hear about all I'd learnt.

"We took advantage of the long winter evenings to discuss how to improve our work. Of course there were a few of us who were a bit conservative, but, in general, we peasants are practical people, and the advantages of mutual aid were clear. We've a firm belief in the saying 'Seeing's believing!' We decided that what needed most attention was better organization of labour and that this could be done if we organized our work all the year round and not just at the busy seasons, that is, if we turned our seasonal team into a permanent, year-round mutual-aid team. And this we did.

"This meant that all the field work could be brought into the general planning, not only the heavy jobs like ploughing, harrowing and sowing or transplanting and harvesting, but the lighter jobs like weeding, cultivating and fertilizing which were suitable jobs for women. Then we could also organize our side-occupations. That meant mainly paper-making. In the seasonal team some members would sometimes want to do paper-making when they were needed for collective work in the fields; there was a conflict of interests. The permanent team ended this conflict of interests. Wang Hsueh-liang, for instance, who was specially good at it, and several others who were not so

---

*Circulated in draft form on December 15, 1951; amended in the light of practical experience and adopted by the Central Committee of the Party on February 15, 1953.

able-bodied, could specialize in it. We could also allow members to specialize in various kinds of field work so that they became quite skilled. The women's work at paper-making could also be brought into the planning. Work points were given to them too. In this way each member could contribute his best efforts. This made us all more efficient and made the team more stable.

"We still used the method of 'fixed points applied flexibly' to assess work, but now we fixed the points to the job not to the member—so many points for weeding a particular field in a set time for instance. If it took longer than set, the member naturally earned less points that day. If he did it badly, the number of points would be reduced. We got quite expert at assessing work this way and we made better use of constructive criticism. Everything was demo-cratically decided by the team members.

"By this time too our eight households had got used to working together, and had developed a good team spirit.

"Members were pretty well satisfied with these arrange-ments and worked well. You'll see that it solved many problems quite satisfactorily. Take for instance the man-power question. This was partly settled in the seasonal MAT. But the permanent MAT was still more helpful.

"Of us eight members only one, Wang Tse-liang, had enough manpower to till his fields by himself. He had 11 *mou* of land and five in his family. Two — he and his brother—were fully able-bodied and the younger brother counted as 'half a man.' They also had implements and a water-wheel. Three of our eight families were quite 'labour poor.' Wang Yuen-liang, for instance, has seven members in his family but only 'one and a half able-bodied men,' he and his son. Four of us eight would have had to hire labour in the busy seasons unless they had the team to help them. Wang Ah-go for instance can't harrow, he's never used a buffalo himself. His son couldn't plant seedlings. And these days you can whistle for hired help. There aren't any landless peasants here any longer. Everyone's got his own land to attend to.

"Then lack of implements: Only one family Wang Keng-chuan had a buffalo, or rather a half share in one. There was only one water-wheel among us and only four had enough implements to till their fields. You can see yourself from this how it paid us to organize mutual aid.

"The weather too in 1952 was as good as it could be.

"That year we got a yield of 420 catties a *mou*, some 40 catties more than in 1951 when we were still in the seasonal MAT.

"Our members were more than satisfied.

"In the seasonal MAT, you see, four of us former poor peasants were living entirely off our incomes. We had no debts and were saving money. But four were still a bit hard up and had to borrow. Now, in the permanent MAT, four of us were free of debts and saving more, two of us were well off and only two were still in difficulties.

"That autumn Wang Pao-yuan went out and bought his family cloth for three cotton suits and pairs of trousers. He bought two more mattocks and sent his child to school. Before liberation he'd been landless, ragged and starving. The first year in the seasonal MAT he'd made enough to buy three cotton padded suits for winter, a rake, a mattock and 35 feet of cloth for quilts—the first new ones they'd had in the family since as long as anyone could remember!

"Wang Tse-liang, also a former landless peasant, bought 20 feet of cloth for the family and a hand water-wheel.

"And so it was with the other MAT members. The two teams worked closely together, passing on experience, helping each other."

In two short years the Tumushan peasants had pulled themselves right up out of the mire of poverty and starvation. Few now thought of being a *tan gan hu* — a work-alone peasant any longer. Their thoughts were on the future.

The transformation of Wang Wen-ken's mutual-aid team into an agricultural producers' co-operative was no easy step to take. Only two years before the peasants of Tumushan had got the land they had dreamt about for generations —land taken from them or their ancestors by the landlords. Now for the first time they had the first little things that made life something more than a grinding toil: decent clothes, enough to eat, houses that really provided shelter, schools for their children. . . . Of the eight poor peasant members of Wang Wen-ken's mutual-aid team, seven were now new middle peasants with an average annual income of 900 catties of grain per person.

It was a big thing to expect them now to say: "Here, I'll put my land into the common pool and we'll jointly decide how to use it for the common good. Pay me only for the labour I put into the common fund and a fair share on my land."

But this step was made easier because they were conscious of the defects of the MAT form of organization. "The MAT can solve problems of labour and use of implements," they said, "but it can't solve problems about the use of land."

In the MAT, each member had his little plot and naturally tried to use it to get a fairly balanced range of crops, as between oil seed and wheat, for instance. Planning on the small scale they did, fields, as often as not were not used to the best advantage either for the individual peasant or the state. Since they worked to such narrow margins, they were also sometimes more than cautious about making innovations in their farming practice. So the pooling of fields and planning their use on a large scale had obvious advantages.

Other MATs had also already made this change and demonstrated its benefits not only in making more efficient use of labour and tools, but in making better use of the land. Eight co-op farms had been formed in Chengling

District in the spring of 1952. One of them, Hsu Kuei-yung's, was practically next door to Tumushan. It had its ups and downs, but it had worked. Its yield was 470 catties a *mou*, despite a setback due to flood. This was 50 catties better than Wang Wen-ken's MAT, a big difference even considering the fact that the MAT's soil was not quite so fertile as the co-op farm's.

The widely publicized experience of these early co-ops was a decisive argument in favour of the change.

Many other MATs in the county were thinking along the same lines. The county Party committee therefore set up a ten-day training class in running MATs and co-op farms. Three Tumushan men attended.

They came back enthusiastic for the co-op. "It will take us to socialism and prosperity for all. Pooled land and better use of land and labour will raise production. In a couple of years there'll be no more needy families!" They brought back concrete suggestions for running the co-op.

Talks and discussion went on for twenty days in meetings, in homes and in the fields. Wang Wen-ken took a leading part in mobilizing support for it. His team was solidly for it. Chu Cheng-teh himself and several others of the best workers in his team were for it. "Since all work in the co-op will be under joint management, those who aren't strong workers can get the most suitable work to do," he said, "and besides I'm strong. There's never been enough work for me to do in the MAT. It's only in the co-op that I'll be able to put all my energy into work that will benefit not only me but all of us."

Wang Chih-shou, the young township Party secretary and a Tumushan man himself, talked of the past and future: "We can't improve life much working alone and working with ancient tools as we do. It's only when we pool our labour and land and form large, strong co-operative farms that we'll be able to use modern farm machines and methods and turn our villages into really big producers and good places to live in. It'll only be then that we'll be able to fit in our plans with those of the country as a whole so that we'll all prosper together."

It was at times of decision like this that the peasants thought particularly of the past: that it was the Communist Party that had led them to freedom and that was now urging them to form co-operative farms. This gave them confidence. Many however still had their doubts.

Party members and the most active peasants worked hard to explain away misgivings.

Wang Ah-go, who before liberation had lived from one debt to another, had been well satisfied with the MAT. His family had got an income equivalent to 4,100 catties of grain in 1951, and 4,300 catties in 1952. Would he do as well in the co-op?

Wang Wen-ken explained that the co-op's yields would be undoubtedly higher than any got in the MAT and, in addition to the dividend on his landshare (about 40 per cent of its standard output)* and the work points he would earn himself, the co-op could find suitable work for his wife (who hitherto did little work in the MAT) and he'd have in addition the produce from his personal allotment. As a matter of fact after the first co-op harvest Wang Ah-go joined the ranks of the well-to-do and for the first time in his life put a deposit in the bank. His wife used often to make a full workday's earnings by collecting grass ash as fertilizer. The feeling that she was really pulling her weight as a producer made a new woman out of her. She became village representative to the local branch of the Women's Democratic Federation.

---

*How landshares are calculated: All land in this co-op farm was graded for its standard output according to its average yield in the past three years, its placing for sunlight and water supply. The owner of land pooled himself proposed which grade his land belonged to. This was confirmed or amended by the co-op committee. The dividend is a percentage of the "standard output" of that grade of land. (40 per cent in the Wang Wen-ken Co-op.)

This question of fertilizer for improving the soil was a key one. Those who could buy more fertilizer got yields 20 and more per cent larger than poorer members.

Wang Tse-liang, for instance, was not as badly off as others even before liberation, so in the MAT he could put more fertilizer on his land and always get a higher yield. Using 160 catties of lime per *mou* he got 390 catties of grain a *mou* on naturally indifferent soil. Wang Yuen-liang on the other hand had fair natural soil but insufficient night soil and could only buy 80 catties of lime per *mou*. He got a yield of only 320 catties a *mou*. Wang Hu-yung, another member, used gypsum, lime, ammonium sulphate and bean-cake fertilizer; he got a yield of 410 catties a *mou*.

All could see that if this went on there could be no talk of all getting prosperous together.

The co-op farm could solve this problem to the benefit of all. Pooled land would mean a common policy of using all fertilizers to the best advantage. All would gain from the higher yields obtainable. Furthermore, some had got to the stage where more fertilizer alone would not increase yields much. More radical measures were needed—better irrigation and cultivation, better seed, etc., that only the co-op could cope with. The co-op could also put in the necessary manpower to dig up pond silt and spread it on the fields. This was one of the best things for the hungry soil. And it was only possible on a big scale in the co-op which would control all the silt-rich ponds and water-ways on the farms, and had the resources to raise the silt to the fields which needed it most. Then, the poorest peasants had usually been given the best soil in the land reform, if this could be well fertilized and irrigated it would bring substantial gains at little extra cost to a co-operative farm.

The co-op would also put an end to bickering over priorities in field work. A 70-*mou* plot of rice land, for instance, must be harvested within a period of a week. The co-op with its available manpower could manage this by careful planning. The MAT never managed to do this. It used to have to hire the help of farmers from neighbouring Fuyang County where they harvest later. This had cost a total of 40 workdays or 240 catties of grain, an average of 10 catties a household. This question of priority often caused tension in the MAT. Each member was anxious to get his fields cropped first. In the co-op it was not a question of "turns" because the crop was owned in common. Pooled fields would mean that labour could be directed wherever it was most needed irrespective of ownership.

When the defects of MATs and the advantages of co-ops had been thoroughly discussed, the honestly expressed doubts of members were answered.

But it was a difficult job to explain away the worries of those who suffered from "ideological" troubles like egoism, individualism and "rich peasantitis," the itch to get rich quick at the expense of others. Such worries were often not even raised in public. In some cases only bitter experience could eradicate them.

There was little need to press the advantages of the co-op on the old and weak. They were obvious. Some old couples had more land than they could handle; the co-op could find them suitable light work and they'd get an income from their landshare. Later, there'd be a welfare fund enough to pay old age benefits.

The young people to a man were eager for it, and many of the oldsters were just as keen. Old Wang Ching-keng said at a meeting: "I'm for socialism. Perhaps I'll never live to see it but I'm willing to work and help you youngsters build it!" The Tumushan peasants formed their co-op farm in the winter of 1952.

How did it come about that this young Wang Wen-ken was so unanimously elected chairman of the new co-op?

When I asked the Tumushan peasants this they answered deliberately as if they had thought this over long ago:

"Wang Wen-ken's always ready to help others. He's always ready for work. He's frank. He bears no malice to anyone."

And when I asked more specifically, they answered: "With Wang Wen-ken, it's this way:

"In the old days, when the Kuomintang was pressganging men during the New Year festival, sometimes there was no time to get up into the hills. Then the only thing to do was to hide in someone's house for a few days. But that was a risky thing for the man that hid you. If you were caught, all right, you'd be pressganged anyway, but he'd be punished for hiding you. But Wang Wen-ken wasn't afraid to help. Just before liberation Loh Ah-yuan hid there. Because he daren't go out, Wen-ken fed him for three days.

"In the land reform Wen-ken was in charge of distributing farm tools. He saw that the best went to others first and then insisted that others decide what he and his family should get.

"When he was hamlet head and saw that Wang Shu-yen's team wasn't running so well, he didn't hesitate to criticize Shu-yen although they're related.

"That's Wang Wen-ken. If it's the public good involved, he's fearless and frank."

"He's a good son and husband. You know his wife was a child-bride, but if other child-brides suffered much in the past Chow Kung-no has never had anything to complain of in Tumushan. You see her father married for a second time and her step-mother wasn't very kind to her. That's how she came to Wen-ken's family. Wen-ken understood his wife's fate. He's never been anything but kind and affectionate."

"He's understanding too to everyone in the co-op."

The oldsters in the co-op say, "Wen-ken's like a son to us."

Such were the opinions of members about Wang Wen-ken.

They knew him as patient in explaining. Once he heard of a new method of seed selection at a meeting called by the district Party committee. He himself was convinced of its benefits, but in deference to doubtful members instead of using it to select half the seed to be used, as originally proposed, he advised that only a small amount should be so selected. The experiment proved a success and the next year the method was adopted by the whole farm.

When the time came to elect model workers in 1955, Wang Wen-ken was unanimously elected by his team and represented the whole co-op at the county conference. At the election meeting they said: "He works well. He's patriotic. He's inventive and full of initiative. He's surely fit to be elected!"

With Wang Wen-ken at their head, Tumushan's peasants were sure that they were led by a man who knew their needs, because their needs were his needs too; who gave all the eagerness and enthusiasm of his youth for them —a young Communist who could lead them along the path which the Party had pointed out to solve the problem of poverty.

Wang Wen-ken is level-headed too. This was a big asset in the first crisis that the new co-op faced.

It was just at this time that many Hsinteng County Party workers and peasant leaders got "dizzy with success." Co-op after co-op was formed, many of which were not too well prepared.

Some peasants, persuaded by over-eager organizers, joined co-ops even though they were not fully convinced of the benefits of joining.

In some such addled co-ops the new committees gaily pooled land, tools, animals and even the household pigs. Reactionary rumour-mongers were quick to paint things in the blackest colours. Some middle and poor peasants, only just thinking of joining MATs, were frankly worried.

The provincial Party committee however quickly took things in hand. There were severe reprimands for the impetuous and explanations to the people of what the real Party policy was. Strict instructions were issued that the principles of voluntariness and mutual benefit must be observed.

The great majority of ill-founded co-ops faded as quickly as they had blossomed and reverted to their former status of MATs, though, as I've related, the over-cautious took the bit in their teeth and several co-ops suffered from it. In common with other co-ops at that time, all the 23 members of the Wang Wen-ken co-op were informed at the general meeting that if they so desired they were free to withdraw immediately.

It was a momentous meeting that showed just how thoroughly the basis for the co-op had been laid. Six, including Wang Hsueh-nan, the one middle peasant of Tumushan, decided to leave. The seventeen who remained formed a tight-knit group defiantly determined to show the backsliders that the co-op would work.

There was deep silence as the six left. Wang Wen-ken looked questioningly at the district committee comrade who had come to the meeting. "That's all right," he muttered, "they'll learn and they'll come back later!"

Why did they leave?

Before liberation Wang Hsueh-nan had owned 14 *mou* of land. His family of five lived frugally but didn't lack for food or clothes. But he paid his landlord 55 per cent of the harvest on the extra four *mou* he rented. Kuomintang price speculations robbed him regularly. Prices went down just as he was ready to sell, and up when he had to buy. But if he was badly exploited he did cherish some hopes of one day doing better. He got a loan from a landlord he was on friendly terms with and bought a buffalo. He became a fairly well-to-do middle peasant. If things went well he hoped he might yet live to be a rich peasant.

Then came liberation and land reform. He looked on with a feeling of mixed satisfaction and apprehension. He saw other middle peasants like Tu Ah-go just over the hill take an active part, closely co-operating with the poor peasants in overthrowing the landlords, helping in the peasants' association and becoming trusted revolutionary workers. He was glad to see the whole grasping lot of landlords and Kuomintang scoundrels cast down. He was relieved to see himself classified as "middle peasant." He had read the Agrarian Reform Law: "Middle peasants in general do not exploit others" and "Land and other properties of middle peasants (including well-to-do middle peasants) shall be protected from infringement." He heard the Party members say: "We must try to bring the middle peasants into a real alliance with the poor peasants." At the end, all his property was intact, farm prices were stable and even raised in relation to industrial goods. There was peace and order.

But he had lost those four *mou* he rented. They had gone to a landless peasant. Now all the peasants had land who could he hire to work on his fields? But this latter problem was solved for him. He joined the work-exchange team and later the mutual-aid team led by Chu Cheng-teh. It was a bit of a "marriage of convenience." He needed at least three people to help him on his 14 *mou* in busy seasons and all the available manpower was in the teams. It was a beneficial marriage however. He exchanged labour with others. He began to get higher yields than ever he had in the past. Free peasants working for mutual aid work better than exploited hired hands! He too helped on the land of other peasant members of the MAT, but it must be admitted that he didn't always work as hard as he might have done. Sometimes he had to swallow his old pride when he had to work for someone who had once been his hired hand and in his displeasure had worked badly, shrugging off criticism of his attitude.

When the question of the co-op farm came up he went along with the rest, but in his heart of hearts he didn't really like the idea. He saw this pooling of land as a divorce from his land rather than as a marriage of convenience for mutual benefit. He saw not so much the future benefits of the co-op as the fact that the land he had always called his own would now be managed by others.

He rarely spoke at meetings, not liking to expose his selfishness, but in private conversations he aired his doubts.

He found some other peasants who had similar unspoken misgivings. Wang Shu-yen, who had once been a *pao* head, had wavered between keenness and apathy in the co-op movement. Shu-yen had hoped to be elected co-op chairman but he had only scraped onto the committee by a few votes. He felt slighted and angry.

When these two got together it was natural that they should air their grievances. "What's the point of rushing into a co-operative when the MAT's doing all right as it is?" was their common thought. Change came hard to them and things were changing fast these days! They felt they should call a halt while they still controlled their little plots fully and could use them as they liked.

One grouse led to another. "In the co-op all the income will go to those who have more labour power. At the beginning of the year they'll settle what dividends we'll get on the land. It'll be lower than the real yield and those who have a bit more land but not much labour will lose out!" A pause, then Wang Hsueh-nan said what he'd been wanting to say from the start: "I've a buffalo. Let's form a MAT of our own. If they want let them go ahead with their co-op!"

That clinched it. At the general meeting Wang Shu-yen walked out and the five others followed suit. They were all poor households but they were misled by Wang Hsueh-nan's black prophecies and their own inability as yet to grasp the full significance of co-operation.

Wang Mei-yung in addition had a simple reason. He was a good ploughman but a bit conservative: "I've ploughed over forty years and I've never been criticized for my work as I've been in this co-op. If you want to plough deeper you get someone else to do it. I'll not stand it!"

Among the dissidents was Wang Kuei-yung.

When Tumushan peasants talk about Wang Kuei-yung it's like talking about the bad boy of the family. In the old days he had hardly enough land to swing a cat on—one-eighth of a *mou*. Every year he had to borrow rice and sank deeper and deeper into poverty. Land reform gave twelve *mou* of land to him and his family of six.

He had prospered in the MAT so that he felt quite well-to-do and self-satisfied. That, combined with his stubborn character, was his undoing.

Wang Hsueh-nan

He wouldn't stand criticism. Telling about why he left the co-op, he complained: "They said my paper wasn't good! Well, perhaps it wasn't good, but it wasn't bad! And they criticized my father and my wife!" (Which wasn't strictly true! His old father had argued fruitlessly for joining the co-op.)

Wang Kuei-yung, former poor peasant but now of middle-peasant status, got hopelessly enmeshed in the doubts and vacillations of a backward individualistic peasant. Looking out over his fields sprouting with winter wheat and yellow flowers of oil beans, he thought:

110

"No one is going to boss me around! Anyway I'll wait and see how things go in the co-op." And he, a poor peasant who should have been in the van of the movement for co-operation, walked out of the meeting at the rear of the most backward peasants in the village! This ill-matched group formed themselves into a mutual-aid team under the leadership of Wang Hsueh-nan.

So it was clear now that the struggle to build the co-op farm in Tumushan wasn't going to be an easy one.

Led by the working-class party the peasants had advanced eagerly and triumphantly from the liberation to the work-exchange teams and mutual-aid teams. Step by step they had learnt the benefit of collective labour.

"The peasant is a toiler as well as a property owner." Their practical sense as toilers had led them on. In the mutual-aid team they still retained full control over their own little individual plots. Not too great a strain had been put on their ingrained sense of property. But now, on joining the co-op, there was a strain and in six of them, subject in one way or another to old ideas, it could not be overcome immediately.

The seventeen who remained in the co-op were more determined than ever to make a go of it. They determined too to win back the waverers. The struggle to make the co-op work well would be at the same time a struggle to prove its worth to all the peasants of Tumushan, to "unite with the middle peasants"; to draw the waverers back onto the straight road of progress and prosperity.

It was not an easy struggle. Old ideas had constantly to be fought and the unfriendly elements, flood and drought, also took a hand against them.

Under Wang Wen-ken's leadership the seventeen new farm co-operators drew on the experience of other co-ops and gave a thorough overhaul to their ways of working.

111

Strict democracy prevailed in settling important points, strict discipline was demanded and observed in carrying out decisions. Since it was a small group, management was made as simple as possible. Chairman Wang had two strong helpers, vice-chairman Wang Hsueh-yung and Tsao Tsai-erh. Young Mrs. Tsao took a special hand in looking after the interests of the increasing number of women who were taking up work in the co-op.

The method of assessing labour by "fixed points applied flexibly" was now used so skilfully that it functioned like a well-run piece-work system.

The Party advised that for the sake of those who pooled more land but had less manpower (and so might not make up an adequate number of work-points at the beginning) the dividend on landshares should not be fixed too low. But on the other hand it should not be too high, as this would discourage those who could contribute the most labour.

In 1953 the ratio of distribution of co-op income was as follows:

Landshares 40%
Payment for labour. 55%
Public fund (reserve and welfare funds). . . 5%

The members pooled money in a fund for production to buy fertilizer, seed, etc. for the common use.

General agreement was also reached on the method of payment for draught animals or larger farm implements used or bought from members. Two small buffaloes owned by members were now sold and money added to buy a full grown animal. Payment for the calves, fixed at the prevailing market rate, was spread over two years with interest added. Paper made and sold to the supply and marketing co-op provided the extra funds. That sleek buffalo, worth nearly two hundred yuan, paraded through the village, was a walking advertisement for the co-op.

112

Each household still retained a small allotment for its personal use. But apart from this the co-op could now plan all the work of the seventeen households and their land as one unit.

A radical plan for improving the land was laid out by the technical committee. This was made up of the best farmers assisted by the newly established state farm of the county and its travelling technicians. Over 30,000 catties of ammonium sulphate, lime and bean-cake fertilizer were bought and laid on with natural fertilizer wherever it did most good. Proper latrines were built at strategic points on the road and in the village. The buffaloes and pigs were properly stalled and compost heaps scientifically cared for. The amount of natural fertilizer thus collected actually increased by a third. Three times as much fertilizer was used. Each field was planted with the crop best suited to it. Five *mou* which had previously been planted with *Ho Huang Hsien* rice gave an increased output of 780 catties when sown with *Teh Kiang Hsien*. Eight *mou* previously left fallow in winter were planted with wheat and rape seed giving an extra 1,500 catties of wheat and 800 catties of vegetable oil seed.

Thirty-five *mou* of the 136 *mou* in the farm was radically improved by irrigation and pond silt. Close planting of rice on 30 per cent of the co-op fields too would give extra yields.

But all this proved to be only the preliminary skirmish for a rich co-op harvest.

First came hail in April—an unheard of calamity! Seedlings were damaged throughout the county. Those in Wang Wen-ken's co-op didn't escape but they were replanted and saved with a strengthened dose of ammonium sulphate. Unable to afford this remedy many unorganized individual peasants had to transplant new seedlings, wasting time and drawing on their reserves.

113

Then drought hit Tumushan. Just when the crops needed rain the red ball of the sun in a burnished sky scorched the fields. At a time when a sleepy summer calm should fill the countryside as the crops ripened, a touch of the old fear crept back into the peasants' hearts. The ponds were drying up. The streams ran dry.

After the tenth rainless day the technical committee grew worried. After waiting a day or so more, they ordered out the small treadle water-wheels and the co-op began to get water from the ponds which had been deepened for just such an emergency. After another eight days it was necessary to bring out every treadle that could be mustered. Seven were repaired and put to work day and night by thirty-five of the strongest men. It was then that the co-op showed its mettle. All hands were thrown into the work, men and women, and the children and old folks did what they could carrying meals to the workers, taking the water in bowls to every drooping plant. Eighty per cent of the co-op's fields were threatened. As the fortieth rainless day dawned, help came from the people's government. The co-op, joining with three mutual-aid teams, was able to borrow a power-driven pump from the state farm, and pumped water from two *li* away where the Hsu Kuei-yung Co-op had repaired their big dam over the Sung Creek. This helped the fields all along the route, those of individual farmers as well as mutual-aid teams. On the forty-seventh day rain fell. Only 1,000 catties of grain were lost. The example of the co-op had encouraged every peasant in the district to battle the drought and save their crops. Many a peasant thought back to what such a drought would have led to in the old days.

It was a great victory for the Tumushan co-op. It reaped a record harvest of 444 catties of grain per *mou*, well beyond that of any mutual-aid team or individual peasant in the district. Stubborn Wang Kuei-yung, working alone, reaped only 380 catties a *mou*.

When the full accounts of the year were posted up they showed that while in 1952 each household in the Wang Wen-ken MAT had received an average of 900 catties of grain in income per person, in 1953, as members of the co-op, they received 1,355 catties each.

Your impetuous doctrinaire will call the peasant "stubborn" and perhaps worse because after an impassioned lecture on the virtues of socialism, large scale collectivization and mechanization of farming he doesn't immediately see how rational all this is and declare himself in favour of collective farms, pool his land and implements and become a disciplined socialist collective farmer. But it is not a question of "stubbornness." The peasant is a man who has been bitterly disappointed many times in the past. He is practical, he is cautious. And the Communist Party, with a magnificent tradition of working-class unity with the peasants, appreciates his sense of the practical and his caution. It is an understanding born of revolutionary friendship. To mobilize the peasants for co-operation means patient, man to man, household to household explanation and proof, not by abstract arguments in concepts difficult for the peasant to understand and grasp, but with practical explanations, by practical results.

The success achieved by the Wang Wen-ken farm co-operative in raising its yields despite natural difficulties was the sort of argument that carried most weight. To the peasants still hesitating to join mutual-aid teams or pondering before voting to turn the team into a co-op, it brought home in immediate practical terms the points that he was now hearing over the radio and in talks, in plays, films and in pamphlets about the General Line of advance to socialism which the Communist Party's Central Committee put before the country in December 1953. Industrialization of the country to make it strong and prosperous . . . the need for more food for the growing cities, more industrial crops for the factories . . . so that more machines could be produced . . . machines to make more machines, machines to produce goods for the people: food, clothing, houses . . . implements for the peasants, new ploughs, harrows, sowers, tractors, combines . . . to pave the way for large-scale, mechanized farming . . . and abundance for all.

They could see how impossible all this would be with a countryside divided up into little farms. The work of tractors and combines seized their imagination. On the cinema screens they saw these machines working on huge Soviet collective farm fields, on the new state farms in China. This brought home to them the incongruousness of such powerful machines and their tiny fields.

Their own experience with the mutual-aid team and co-op farm linked up at that point with this general picture: Pool the labour power, the animals, and implements, pool the fields; learn how to manage things in common; improve the land *mou* by *mou*; raise yields; build up experience; learn to perfect co-operation and the habit of it. . . .

Thus the practical success of the Wang Wen-ken Co-op encouraged four mutual-aid teams in the immediate neighbourhood to become co-ops. Practically all of the 145 households in the township were either in co-ops or mutual-aid teams now.

And what of middle peasant Wang Hsueh-nan? His mutual-aid team, formed of such individualists, led a stormy existence. Hardly had it got going when Wang Kuei-yung quarrelled with his fellow members and withdrew in high dudgeon. In the harvest season interminable bickering led to the break-up of the team as each insisted that his crop be taken in first. Yet such was the magic of the MAT formula even in the work they did do together, they got yields of up to 396 catties per *mou*, a sizable increase over 1952.

It was a bitter victory however. Wang Wen-ken's co-op farm battling against just the same difficulties as they, had topped their best yields by 48 catties a *mou*! This made Wang Hsueh-nan think again. For all its faults from his point of view the co-op was working and getting better yields than he could get even in a team under his own direction! Bitterest pill was that the *mou* of land the co-op had enriched with silt just before he withdrew gave a yield of 380 catties against its former 280.

Taking the advice of the Party the ill-matched six decided to form their own little co-op!

The Wang Wen-ken Co-op entered 1954 with that grand feeling that "this is the year!"

It was a sign of the growing political consciousness of Tumushan that two more peasants were accepted into the Communist Party that year, raising the number of Party members to four. Problems of management were getting more complex as the co-op took on more tasks, but members became steadily more experienced, more closely knit as a community, and took things in their stride. They continued to develop the methods that had brought success in 1953. There was a still more efficient division of labour. Even secondary tasks now had their specialists. More dry land was transformed into more fertile irrigated soil. More silt and fertilizer was used to improve soil. Less land was allowed to lie fallow in the winter; it was put to wheat, vegetable oil crops or grass fertilizer.

Close planting, deep ploughing and seed selection were carried through systematically. Each gave its quota of increased yield. Planting wheat in rows on 80 per cent of the co-op fields gave an estimated increase of 10 per cent in yield over the former method of planting wheat in small, spaced-out clumps.

Better division of labour and increased investments increased the output of paper. In 1953 the co-op made 2,822 blocks of paper (each of a 1,000 sheets) worth 1.1 yuan each. In 1954 it made 3,000 blocks, each worth 1.25 yuan, a net gain of nearly 650 yuan.

In 1954, the co-op once more beat off the attacks of unfriendly nature. Several times that year flood damaged the crop. The seedlings were inundated in March. Co-op members worked through the night cleaning the heavy mud off the tender shoots and stood them upright and clean again. Several times more they were damaged. New seedlings had to be put in from reserves to replace those fatally damaged. Extra seedlings had to be bought from the reserves of other co-ops. Over 100 workdays went on this work — but the crop was saved.

The yield in the autumn of 1954 was 457 catties a *mou* (compared to 444 in 1953) and the average income per person rose to 1,500 catties of grain. The proportion of income that went to labour was increased from 40 to 42 per cent.

Chu Cheng-teh was right. In the co-op he was a tower of strength. He was a champion at transplanting — winning a prize for it, and at ploughing and harrowing, digging and carrying. He practically doubled his old income in the mutual-aid team, earning nearly 5,000 catties in 1953 and nearly 6,500 in 1954.

This growing prosperity was general. All except three of the original 17 in the Wang Wen-ken Co-op were now middle peasants in status. There were eleven well-to-do households, the rest had enough to spend and small savings. Only one was still in difficulties: Wang Keng-chuan, who had been sick for six months in 1953 and for three months in 1954.

The co-op spent most of its public funds in 1953-54 to buy four new ploughs, two water-wheels, three carts and equipment for increasing its output of paper. Its members bought much needed goods: 8 mosquito nets, 12 quilts, 12 woollen sweaters, 145 yards of cloth, five good quality cotton twill suits, and four wheelbarrows. Two new houses were built, the smaller costing 500 yuan. Several were repaired and enlarged. Many thermos bottles and flashlights were bought.

Every young man acquired a fountain pen and notebook — essential in these days of democratic meetings and study.

All this also adds up to the fact that the members of the co-op can make a progressively larger contribution to the country. The grain tax was promptly paid. In 1953, they sold 15,000 catties of grain to the state under the unified purchase and supply of grain plan. In 1954, they sold the state 23,500 catties of grain as well as vegetable oil of which China has a growing need.

After that triumphant harvest and especially after the study of the General Line of the Party for the transition to socialism, there was a strong movement to link up with the best co-op of the village. Two other co-ops joined with Wang Wen-ken's, to form a big co-op of 62 households.

Among the mergers was middle peasant Wang Hsueh-nan's co-op.

It hadn't been a brilliant success, but it had been a valuable school of experience for its members. It had been helped economically and politically by the co-operative "network" which the village co-operators had formed to coordinate the work of the various MATs and co-ops. It had also studied the General Line. That helped a lot. Wang Hsueh-nan began to see more clearly that the only way of advance for the peasant now — whether hired labourer, poor peasant or middle peasant of the past — was through co-operatives to strong, well-run mechanized farms. Only that could solve the problem of poverty once and for all.

There was no way back to the past and you couldn't stand still. Furthermore the co-op really did work and was more efficient than he could ever be on his own. It was the yield that moved him specially. His co-op had increased its yield to 420 catties a *mou*, but the Wang Wen-ken Co-op, better run than his, was still ahead — 457 catties a *mou*!

That settled it! He and all his co-op unanimously voted to merge.

And Wang Kuei-yung? From morning till night there was argument in his house, because his wife and his father wanted to rejoin the co-op and he wouldn't. Then his house, the strong house his grandad had built, fell in. And he had to borrow money, just as he had in the past, while former poor peasants, now co-op members, were putting their first savings in the bank! And finally he'd only got a yield of 360 catties a *mou*, a proper work-alone yield! That clinched it! He too saw light and rejoined amid general rejoicing.

When I left Tumushan in 1955 the big co-op was already formed. It had 460 *mou* of land and its members were divided into four teams, with most of the Tumushan people forming one team. Work was in full swing. On the basis of improvements already made to their land they were going to introduce the double crop and high yield, late crop system of cultivation on half their land. This they expected would give an average yield of 475 catties a *mou* in 1955.

With bigger reserves of manpower (235 men and women) they had put 2,000 of a total of 4,400 workdays into a scheme to take soil from fields to build a much needed dyke on the Sung Creek and at the same time turn these same formerly dry fields into low-lying irrigated ones. In this way 25 *mou* would be improved as part of the plan to increase the output of rice by 10,800 catties.

Serious faced Wang Hsueh-yung and his jolly wife, his brother and wife, younger brother and mother typify the spirit and achievements of the Tumushan co-operators.

Their simple house — grandfather built it a century ago — had been repaired and newly painted. And there was money in the bank and a 200 yuan stock of timber ready there alongside to build a brand-new house for the growing family. They are well fed and well clothed. And this after only five years of co-operation, including two in the co-op.

Before liberation they had less than one *mou* between them. They rented another eight *mou* from a landlord and paid 70 per cent of the crop in rent. That left 1,000 catties for all their back-breaking toil. They cut firewood, hired themselves out and so raised another 2,000 catties of grain. This was still not enough, so in the spring famine they ate the tender buds of trees or the roots of grass fertilizer. They had no warm clothes and only one quilt for the six of them. To let the youngsters have it Hsueh-yung used to sleep with bachelor friends.

It's no wonder they literally glow with enthusiasm as they compare the past with today. Last year in the co-op they earned 16,200 catties of grain. In 1951 in the seasonal MAT they earned 6,000 catties; in the permanent MAT they earned 8,000, in 1953 in the co-op, 10,000.

Over two-thirds of last year's income was payment for work, the rest was their landshare dividend, the harvest from their allotment and the proceeds of the pig they raised and sold.

Twenty per cent of their income went on investments in the co-op (mainly for paper-making, a recurring investment credited to their account), for the purchase of tools and their agricultural tax (1,000 catties). Most of the other 80 per cent went on living expenses (13,200 catties of grain a year at 1,100 catties a month).

Food is still the biggest item of expenditure, about 50 yuan a month. They eat meat two or three times a month. Last autumn (1954) they spent 70 yuan on clothes and an equal sum the autumn before. They have bought four new quilts. They also set aside a sum for cigarettes, tea and sweets for the two new babies, toothbrushes, paste, soap and face cream and such like for the women. These items usually tot up to 7 yuan a month.

When we had settled these items, there was a chorus from the assembled family of: "Don't forget younger brother is studying at primary school!" That adds another 10 yuan a year.

"He's doing well," said Wang Hsueh-yung. "He's sixteen — a bit old for primary school, but he had no chance to go to school before. He works hard and he got a prize recently."

What they saved after this went to buy the timber for the new house.

"We peasants have gained all round. In the old days the price of rice dropped just as soon as the crops came in. Then a yard of cloth cost around two yuan. Now the price of rice is set and steady. A yard of cloth costs about one yuan.

"The people's government also keeps a kind eye on the price of our paper. We get a better price for it now.

"The government scheme to purchase all our surplus stocks of rice and hold reserves here in the village in case of need, works for us too. In the old days we peasants said:

> Keep grain for natural calamities;
> Keep a son for your old age!

Those ideas are already out of date. Now we keep just enough for our needs and sell the rest to the government which stores it for us. If our own stocks run out we can buy back some from the government at the same price we were paid for it.

"Then there's medical treatment in the clinic. Doctor's fees and medicines are still a bit expensive sometimes, but when we need them, they're right there. Mobile teams come to inoculate the babies free and so is ordinary first aid. We see the cinema now and we hear the broadcasts every day from the county town, news and music and opera. We've a new library in the co-op.

"All this makes a big difference. We used to have plenty of family quarrels in the old days. Worries got on our nerves. But we're not naturally that way. Now we've not had a tiff for five years."

There was a meditative pause in the talk at that. And in the silence we heard a passionate voice in the next room say: "I'll never leave you. . . ." No one seemed surprised but me. In answer to my enquiring looks I was told: "That's Ho Hsi-erh. She's just joined the dramatic group!"

Village Clinic

MAKING UP LOST DAYS

An early spring drizzle was drenching the Chekiang countryside. Low clouds scudded over the evening sky, veiling the surrounding mountains in mist. The brook gurgled loudly and the water flowed with anxious urgency from paddy field to paddy field.

Wearing coira-palm raincoats and broad hats of plaited bamboo, carrying umbrellas of bamboo and oiled paper as their ancestors have done for centuries, or clad in new-fashioned macintoshes or oil-skins, with galoshes and metal-ribbed umbrellas, the members of the Tumushan Co-operative Farm made their way to the general meeting. It was being held in one of the larger farmhouses.

Each household in the co-operative had sent at least one representative and some had sent two or three. Soon about eighty people, not counting the children, were gathered under the bright circle of light shed by a purring paraffin lamp. There was no set order for seating. Groups sat talking quietly together. Mothers nursed their babies in the shadows. Several people listened to the broadcast from the county town, which was passing on the methods used by the best co-ops for looking after buffaloes. The talk was followed by excerpts from the popular Shao-hsing opera, *Liang Shan-po and Chu Ying-tai*, the Butterfly Lovers.

It was all very informal. The chairman didn't even call for order, but began to speak from the middle of the room. The talking immediately died down.

He opened with some good news: "We have already turned ten *mou* of dry land into irrigated fields!" There was a stir of satisfaction, which he checked. "Wait a bit!

The next news is not so good. We haven't fulfilled our work plan since the New Year festival. A lot of us have been turning up to work late. Now we've got to get over that holiday feeling and make up for the time we've lost!"

He spoke about some of the attitudes which he thought were hindering the work:

"I know that some of you younger ones who volunteered for the People's Liberation Army feel disappointed that you weren't accepted. But you shouldn't let that affect your job. Remember, there are thousands volunteering, and they can't all be taken. If you really want to help your country you'll work harder than ever to make our farm programme succeed.

"Then some people have apparently been thinking that since the co-op has sixty-two households to do the work, they wouldn't be missed if they took an occasional day off. But what would happen if we all acted like that?"

He called on everyone, the committee members in particular, to combat wrong ideas such as these and to talk to everybody about the proper attitude towards work in a co-operative.

The next item on the agenda was the nomination of delegates to attend a model workers' conference shortly to be held in the county town. Each team was asked to select its best workers to represent the co-op on this important occasion. "Don't forget the boys who mind the buffaloes," reminded the chairman. "The way these animals do their work this spring depends on how well they were taken care of during the winter."

The Communist Party secretary added a word about the standards that should be used for selecting the best team members. "I suggest that they should be the same as usual — good work, keenness in studying technique, care for co-op property and the public interest, and a creative attitude to work."

125

The meeting assented, and immediately broke up into groups. Each group consisted of one of the small teams, and lively discussions began on the nominations.

Snatches of conversation were heard from the first team, where someone had been cited as a "good worker."

"What sort of a good worker is it who pays no attention at production meetings!" said a scathing voice. "All he thinks of is accumulating work-points to increase his own earnings."

The recommendation was rejected after a sporadic defence on the part of the nominator.

The buffalo boys? Here the team encountered a difficult problem. All the buffaloes were well looked after — the three buffalo boys had organized themselves into a mutual-aid group, so nobody could say which was best. After some debate, all three were nominated.

The discussion began to narrow. Wang Wen-ken was nominated unanimously. He was ill at the moment and was not present, or he would have heard them say: "Old Wang is a good worker . . . he's a good patriot — thinks of the country and puts other people's interests before his own . . . inventive, too. He must be nominated."

"Anyone else?" asked Wang Hsueh-yung, who was leading the discussion.

"You yourself!" said someone.

While he was being discussed, Wang Hsueh-yung sat silent, holding his baby in his arms. He had taken an animated part in the discussion up to that point but now his face showed no expression, either of false modesty or eagerness.

"A good worker! He's been a first-rate leader while Wen-ken's been away!"

There was no dissent. The decision came very quickly. "Nominated!"

Eventually all the teams ended their discussions, and one by one they reported back to the general meeting. The second team nominated their accountant and, to the surprise of the rest, cited a man called Yeh who until recently had been quite well-known as one of the laziest members. Since the New Year he had turned over a new leaf and had washed ten blocks of pulp for the paper which the co-op manufactures as a cottage industry. Team No. 2 also commended one of their buffalo boys, criticized his partner for displaying bad temper, and warmly mentioned another member who had taken less than the agreed number of days off for the New Year.

The third team nominated Leh Chung, its leader: "He takes care of the whole team like a father." And they took the opportunity to censure Chin Kung-to, one of the rank-and-file, for "plain, downright laziness!" He had not worked a single one of the thirteen days since the New Year festival had ended, preferring odd jobs of barbering to field work. Someone had composed a satirical rhyme about him:

> He gets a headache when there is a meeting
> He dozes when the meeting makes a start
> And when it comes to working
> Then his stomach starts a-hurting
> Work is not a thing that Kung-to has at heart!

The fourth team also nominated its team leader, and, like Team No. 1, censured a member whose only aim was to win work-points. This caused general laughter because each team seemed to have someone like this.

The Party secretary summed up the meeting with a very earnest speech. He reminded the members of the importance of the winter's work, particularly the paper-making. The co-operative had already received a substantial advance payment on the winter's output of paper from the supply and marketing co-operative.

"We are using this money to buy fertilizer, and we need every bit of it if we are to carry out our plan to reap two rice crops this year. So a great deal depends on the amount of paper we turn out now.

"We overfulfilled our quota in December, but the slacking off this month after the festival has set us back badly. We all agreed that we would start work after the five days' holiday, but a lot of people took two and even three days extra. This lost us over two hundred workdays.

"Then we agreed to turn 25 *mou* of dry field into irrigated land as part of our plan to grow an extra 10,800 catties of rice this year. We haven't half finished the job yet!"

He paused for a moment. Everyone was listening intently. The steady drip of the rain could be heard outside, warning them that precious time must not be wasted if the first quarter's plan was to be fulfilled.

"Better discipline is the answer," he said. "That, and greater attention to study. Our general education and political understanding both need a lot of improvement."

A voice from the floor proposed that the teams should meet the following evening to work out plans for making up the time lost. There was general acceptance.

The meeting of Team No. 1 which was held next evening was just as informal as the general meeting. The little downstairs room was crowded. The oil lamp burning on the table lit up the circle of faces directly around it; the rest of the room was in deep shadow. On the wall an incongruously large clock, a "fruit of the land reform" (when the surplus property of the landlords was divided among the peasants) ticked away between two red scrolls with "happiness" symbols on them.

The discussion moved naturally from point to point. It resembled not so much a meeting as a family discussion. It began with the calculation of the number of lost days' work that had to be made up, how much manpower was available, and how much each person could contribute.

The young woman playwright from the Hangchow Writers' Association, who was staying in the village for a

128

Bamboo rafting on the Sung, Hsinteng County

Setting out rice seedlings

Comrade Chin (*right*), Secretary of the Hsinteng County Communist Party Committee

A co-op farm team weeding a paddy field

Ploughing

Hsu Kuei-yung and a girl county official

Ho Hsi-erh (the Chinese character means "happiness")

Tsao Tsai-erh separating sheets of damp paper

Kindergarten

Outside a Tumushan cottage

A co-op farm team checks up work-points

Wang Wen-ken and the Party secretary at Tumushan (*2nd and 3rd left*)

Pien Chu-shen holds up his co-op's appeal to ban the atom bomb

A group of Chengling District cadres

Wong Kuan-yu, Secretary of the Chengling District Communist Party Committee

School sports in Hsinteng county town

few months to get material for a play, sat by the team's recorder and manipulated the abacus expertly for him, while he wrote down her totals. She seemed quite at home among the peasants; she had worked in touring theatrical groups going around the countryside since liberation, and had taken part in the land reform.

Only fourteen members out of the team of seventeen were present. The other three were sick. That meant harder work for the remainder, and more than one of them spoke ruefully about the lost days.

"I really meant to start work again on the fourth," said one. "But the visitors kept on arriving. What could I do?"

Suggestions were put forward for remedying the situation. Someone proposed adding an extra half-hour morning and evening to the day's work. Another calculated that they could save perhaps 120 workdays if they asked all the members to lend their wheelbarrows to shift the straw for paper-making, instead of using carrying poles. Time could be saved by moving the lime fertilizer in this way too.

Wang Hsueh-yung, the team leader, proposed that each man should promise to make four extra blocks of pulp before the end of the present quarter. Several voices murmured in protest.

"Four! We'll never manage it!"

Wang Hsueh-yung turned, as he often did, to consult an old grizzled farmer sitting beside him. Wise and experienced, he was a member of the technical committee. He pondered for a moment, then said: "It can be done!"

That settled it.

"If the rain goes on much longer, we'll have to concentrate on paper-making for a while," commented the woman writer. There was a chorus of assent.

"If it goes on much longer, we'll have to give a workday for prayer to get the heavenly sluice-gates closed!" added a voice, and everyone laughed.

"The very first fine day that comes, we must get the fertilizer spread," said the recorder. "How many workdays will it take?"

Several people spoke at once. "Ten!" said some, while others said eight or nine.

"What is it to be?" asked the recorder, his pen poised over the record-book. "Don't forget we are behindhand!"

"All right, then — eight!"

Finally came the allocation of work, with a definite quota for each worker, and a definite number of work-points for each job. Whether it was washing paper-pulp or spreading fertilizer, or doing a job on a wet field or a dry one, each task was clearly visualized and the number of points decided with no more than a minute's discussion. A year or two ago, when these people were new to co-operative work, matters like this sometimes gave rise to lengthy wrangles. Now that the teams have been working together and holding short production meetings almost every day, things are settled swiftly and efficiently.

An assessment of four and a half points was suggested for laying fertilizer on a certain field.

"I think four is enough," said a team member. "Four points — it's half a good day's work."

"Maybe you think you could do it!" came the ironic rejoinder. "You try to do it in half a workday yourself, if you think it's so easy!"

The recorder glanced at the wise old farmer, who shook his head.

"Four and a half, then!" said the recorder. And he wrote it down.

Point by point the meeting went on, until everything was settled. The babies had dropped off to sleep and their mothers had come and carried them to bed. One of the buffalo boys curled himself drowsily in the big bamboo armchair. Members of other teams who had finished their business dropped in to see how things were going and report on what they had decided.

The co-op had shaken off that after-the-holiday feeling. Resolve had been strengthened. The job was in hand. Looking at those faces — ruddy with youth and health or brown and leathery, time-worn and wise; looking at those hands, strong, sinewy and capable — how was it possible to doubt that these sturdy folk would fulfil their plan!

Meeting of the Small Team

Fate rained blow after blow on Chen Shih-teh until he was punch-drunk. He was beaten to his knees. His own father became the hand of fate. He beat Chen Shih-teh in the fits of fury that wracked him, the fury of frustration, of nerve-wracking poverty. He beat his grandson and the starved child died from the blows. In a fit of remorse the old man fell ill and died too.

One day while Chen Shih-teh was out chopping firewood in the hills, Kuomintang troops, scouring the village for loot and women, dragged his wife screaming from the house. No one dared try to stop them. As they were marching her across the bridge, she broke loose from them and threw herself into the water. Like hooligans tormenting a stray cat, they dragged her dripping out of the water and beat her within an inch of her life. She never recovered from this and died soon after.

Chen Shih-teh was left alone, with no family, no land, no home. The landlord he worked for as a hired labourer encouraged him to build a shack of straw and branches to live in, but it wasn't long before he was turned out of this and the landlord used it to stable his buffalo.

Then Chen Shih-teh rented a corner of a shed from neighbours. Moving wasn't difficult. All he had was the worn clothes on his back; a tattered quilt, a chopper and a few other odds and ends that could be carried on one end of a bamboo pole.

He worked for another landlord, Chiu, a regular vulture of a woman. There was no one else to work for but the landlords, and if one was a vulture then the other was a tiger, or worse. He got a single meal a day and sometimes not that, of grain mash and left-overs shared with the pigs.

Landlord Chiu called this charity and as a big concession promised him forty dollars a year.

At the end of the year, just before the Spring Festival, he got ten of these dollars. Timidly, plucking up all his courage, he asked for the rest. There was an explosion of landlord wrath such as even he did not expect. He was accused of thievery and rascality, black ingratitude and communism. He was taken to town and thrown into the county lock-up. He lay there for five months till he fell sick. Not wanting to have him die on their hands, the Kuomintang jail authorities released him.

He crawled back along the road to Tumushan, more dead than alive.

That was the way liberation found him nearing his sixtieth year.

Gradually he got back his health. He couldn't take part in the first work-exchange group as he had no land (this was just before the land reform) so he hired himself out to another landlord. But this time he got real wages and the food was better. It was after the campaign to overthrow the rural tyrants; that was one reason. Life was still hard, but he had heard that the people's government was going to see to it that the peasants got back their land. He lived on that promise and it gave him strength. Perhaps the landlord had heard it too. And that promise came true. In the great land reform Chen Shih-teh got just over two *mou* of land. Some of it was a hillside plot with a low yield, but more than a *mou* of it was good, fertile valley land given him by unanimous consent because he was so poor and had suffered so bitterly in the past. He got a sickle and a matchet as well. They offered him a room, but this was too far away from his old neighbours and he preferred to stay where he was in Tumushan.

When he is asked: "What did you do in the land reform?" Chen Shih-teh hangs his head. The other villagers at the accusation meeting told everything they knew about the landlords' crimes. They even told about how Chen Shih-teh had been mistreated. But he himself, although they all called on him to speak, only stood there as if numbed, silent, not knowing what to say.

It was not easy even after land reform. He had land, but not enough implements and no buffalo. But he had his strength and farming experience to exchange with others. He joined the first work-exchange team set up after the land reform in Tumushan.

The other team members knew that he hadn't much labour to exchange, still they classified him as a "half manpower." Now the slogan rang true: "All the Peasants Are One Family!" Half manpower or less, Chen Shih-teh had been one of the most exploited in the old society. In the new China the peasants would see to it that he wouldn't stand in need.

That year there was a drought, but the team provided him with a water-wheel and brought water to his fields just as they did to those of every other member. Never before had he worked so happily. He couldn't do the heavy work like ploughing, harrowing or transplanting seedlings, but he was painstaking at weeding and hoeing, slow but thorough. In the seasonal mutual-aid team at first he was still a "half manpower," but his worries fled. Fate began to smile on him. In the team, when others lost their tempers over what they considered were unjust assessments of their labour or whose field should be harvested first, Chen found tongue to remind them of the old days and plead for good fellowship, for a spirit of give and take.

That year he got nearly 500 catties of rice from his land, the first crop he had ever raised on his own land in 50 years of farming. He paid off his debts, stacked the rest away and took his little bag of "Victory Grain"* punctually and happily to the state granaries.

_____
*Agricultural tax.

Chen Shih-teh was one of the first to join the permanent mutual-aid team. He worked hard no matter on whose field he was assigned to work. With the help of the team that year he raised 500 catties of rice and the equivalent of 100 more in beans and turnips, vegetable oil seed and wheat. It was more than the landlord used to get on that land. He bought a new cover for his worn quilt, a new cotton suit and a mat to dry his grain on.

When the question came up of forming a farming co-operative in 1952, Chen Shih-teh was no longer silent. He spoke at meetings; he argued for the co-op in the cottages and in the fields. Wang Wen-ken, the team leader, who took the initiative in proposing the change, had no more ardent helper.

It was when the co-op was formed that Chen Shih-teh became a buffalo boy. The co-op, which now controlled all the labour of its members and managed all their land and side-occupations in common, could find suitable work for all, men and women, old and young. As buffalo boy he got 75 workdays to his credit. At eight points a workday that meant over 700 catties of grain a year. With his landshare at 200 catties and points for other odd jobs making another 200 catties, he earned altogether over 1,100 catties of grain that year.

He was as conscientious as ever; a model for many stronger than himself. One day he was given a job of weeding the paths on the boundaries between the paddy fields. It was roughly assessed beforehand at two and a half work-points. But when it was finished he asked for

Chen Shih-teh

five points. This caused quite a stir at the production meeting that evening and some members said that even if it were done extra well it couldn't be worth more than three to four at the most. But Wang Ching-shui passed the place as he was carrying co-op produce to town and was so impressed with the job Chen Shih-teh had done that that same evening he proposed that the points given should be raised to the full five.

That winter Chen Shih-teh slept in perfect bliss for the first time in his life. He had sold all his surplus grain to the state and bought himself a splendid coffin.* A great load was lifted from his heart as he followed it home from Hsinteng Town. At last a place for his final rest was ready and waiting for him. It was of polished pine, of great boards four inches thick. On the head board was written the single character *Fu*—Happiness.

He installed it himself in the ancestral temple to the right of the tabernacle. (He had to move aside some of the co-op's lime fertilizer which was stored there, shovelling it well back so it wouldn't get wetted by the rain.) Among all the coffins there, waiting and ready for the other lucky oldsters of the village, it was the newest, shiniest and finest — a coffin made by carpenters after the liberation, good honest fellows, who had taken part in the movement against the "five dishonest practices" of merchants, and had formed a co-operative; none of your shoddy, pre-liberation stuff!

Life smiles more and more broadly on Chen Shih-teh. His yearly income has steadily increased. He has bought himself a new pair of trousers and a new mattock and (since he paid off for the coffin) a new coira-palm raincoat.

"What would I have if it wasn't for the co-op!" he cries, warming to his favourite subject. "Others may have

---

* It is a settled tradition among the old in China, to prepare their own coffins in plenty of time.

wrong ideas but I know what's good for me and for all the peasants.

"I'll go into a socialist collective farm too. Socialism is good. It means that for us old 'uns, old age won't be a time of misery. Let's build it soon! Work together, that's socialism!

"I've sold all the grain I could to the state. I sold 374 catties of rice and paid my grain tax promptly. I kept 200 catties by me. That's not quite enough, but I'll make up for it with more beans and potatoes. They're good to eat too. I starved in the old days for the landlord. Certainly I can eat a little less rice and more potatoes* if it's for the people! I'm an old man now, I don't need much. It's the little I can do to help build socialism. It'll help to liberate Taiwan!"

Chen Shih-teh is a model buffalo boy. He's been awarded a prize for his good work in looking after his buffalo.

Down in the ancestral temple his coffin stands new and shiny, but it's gathering a bit of dust on top. He's stopped going down there, as he used to, to brush it up.

The last time I saw him sitting astride the buffalo, in his straw hat and coira-palm armour against the rain, he was deep in thought.

"What are you thinking about, Chen Shih-teh?" I asked.

He answered slowly: "Well, to tell the truth, I'm think-ing of building a house to live in!"

---

*Potatoes are still not very popular among the peasants who consider them much inferior to rice.

The recipe for prosperity through co-operation has an important, an essential ingredient: "Let the women be emancipated and enter your comradeship as equal partners!"

One evening when she had cleared up after the evening meal and sat down to give her baby his last feed, Tsao Tsai-erh told me how that ingredient was added to the life and work of Tumushan.

Tsao Tsai-erh is one of the most progressive and active young matrons of the hamlet and one of the prettiest too. It did you good to see her intelligent face and her lively eyes. She wore a blue padded cotton jacket, trousers of a darker colour, pink stockings and black slippers. Her hair was cut to her shoulders and framed her face in rich, glossy waves.

She had been named Radiant Child. It was an appropriate name for her life after liberation, but it was a cruel mockery of her real childhood. There had been little radiance in that childhood except such as her naturally happy nature snatched from the misery of constant hunger and nagging winter cold. And as she grew up, life became even harder. Children at least shared with the menfolk whatever there was to eat in the home. Grown girls, like all the womenfolk of these hungry villages under the Kuomintang, always took second place to the men.

There was a decided note of feminist militancy as Tsao Tsai-erh told me about that past!

"In those days women were oppressed by the menfolk as well as by the landlords! They ate first because, it was said, 'the men do the work.' They seemed to forget that we had all the housework to do, as well as look after the babies and help with the paper-making!

"But the women never dreamt of breaking that rule. It wouldn't cross your mind even, no matter how hungry you were, to eat until the menfolk came back of an evening. If you had dared to take anything out of the dish or sat down at table before them there'd have been a row. It would have been the talk of the village. You'd have been scolded by your husband and your mother-in-law. And if you had answered back and your mother-in-law had beaten you, your husband would have had to beat you too, to show he was a filial son!

"Even when there was enough food on the table for everyone, young girls and wives had a limit of two bowls of rice. Even to take a second bowl was going rather far. Two bowls and then the mother-in-law would take the rice pot over to the other side of the table!

"You know, most women never knew what money was to handle! Husbands kept all the family accounts. You had to ask them for every cent you spent and payments above a few cents were done by them anyway. I don't suppose nine out of ten of us women could have recognized a big banknote if you'd shown it to us. Most of us couldn't read, you see.

"I hear that in most countries women dress better than men. But with us it was different. The men wore better clothes than the women. We didn't mind that if it was a case of them having to be warmly dressed so they could do their work. But it wasn't only that, it was part of the general way women were always put in the second place.

"I've often asked myself why the women were treated so. Good husbands like mine behaved better to their wives than others, but even they dared not go too far against the old customs. I can see now that it's true that it all had something to do with feudalism, as I've been told, and I suppose it was one way of keeping us poor peasants poor.

"Before the liberation women weren't allowed to work in the fields. This was a big hardship for poor families with little manpower. It wasn't considered proper for women to expose any part of the body except the face and hands. That's why we all wore slippers and stockings and didn't dare roll up the ends of our trousers to work in the wet fields. All we were allowed to do was a little bit of light work in the garden if we had one, or help with separating the damp sheets of paper and taking them out to dry. No matter what happened, drought or flood, we couldn't go out to help the menfolk save the crops!

"Would you believe it—when the cadres called on us women to help in the fields so that we could help increase production, and become emancipated, there were some old fogies here who said that the grain we raised would surely shrivel up and if it didn't shrivel up it was nothing but unclean grain anyway!"

Several other women had come in when they heard that we were discussing the "woman question." They were the wife of the young township branch Party secretary, a Youth League member; her mother-in-law, Ah Ma, kindly faced and young in spirit, always ready for laughter despite her mature years, and another girl in the Youth League with a handsome round face, bold and confident. They were quick to interject comments and recollections to fill out the story.

Ah Ma was a mine of information on the old days.

"Marriages were not made like they are today. They were all fixed by the parents and the go-betweens. Families made the first choice, and I suppose they tried to do the best for their children, but the final choice depended on the horoscopes of the pair. If these were propitious then you were married. You never saw your husband till you were

140

Farmstead Kitchen.—

married to him. Some of us were lucky and some of us were not so lucky!"

And there was no doubt from her face that she had been one of the lucky ones.

"No girl dared say she preferred any special partner. If the idea ever crossed their minds I'm sure it would have been beaten out of them. The boys were married off at 18 and the girls at 16. Parents, you see, were eager to have grandchildren so as to have someone to look after them in their old age. Most of the older women here, as a matter of fact, were child-brides. You see, marriages in those days were expensive affairs. Besides the presents that had to be exchanged between the families, and the dowry, there were presents for the go-betweens and you had to invite all the important relatives on both sides to the ceremony even if it ran your neck deep in debt. And you had to be particularly careful to invite those that didn't like you! If they weren't invited they might say that the ceremonies hadn't been properly carried out and the marriage wasn't legal. That could cause no end of scandal. Oh, what a time it was in those days!"

The young girls were hearing some of this for the first time just as I was, and they were round-eyed with interest. What they had escaped!

"That's why there were child-brides. That kind of marriage didn't need a big marriage feast. Just a few clothes and presents, that was all—at least, so far as the marriage ceremony was concerned. Child-brides were taken into poor families and brought up by them until they were of really marriageable age. Many of them led a bitter life.

"Wong Pao-kun was a child-bride. She was ten then and her husband was 11 years older. She was terribly oppressed. When she brought firewood back from the hills she'd have to show her mother-in-law what she'd gathered. If the old lady was satisfied, then she'd get food—just the rice left-overs, that had stuck to the sides of the pot, softened with hot water. If the old lady thought she hadn't brought back enough, then all she'd get was a beating. And her husband would have to beat her too!

"There were all sorts of strict rules we women had to obey. We never knew the reason for a lot of them. Even at the New Year festival, when all the men went out visiting, the women had to stay at home. They weren't allowed to go out of the house or courtyard until eight days after the festival. When we asked why, we were told that if anyone saw a woman out before that time he would sicken and die. As a special treat, if the head of the family allowed it, young wives were allowed to go and visit their parents on the fifteenth day. This was also just about the time when we used to have three days of opera at the temple theatre. On the first two days only the men went. On the third day some of the women were allowed to go. But if you went you didn't dare walk around or even look around to see what was happening. You had to keep your eyes on the ground or fixed on the stage. I remember one girl who was sitting there and waved to her mother when she saw her come in. Her mother-in-law took her back home that instant."

The Party secretary's mother paused and laughed quietly to herself at some thought.

"In all the days before liberation—and I'm forty now— I never went once to the county town!"

And the county town is just a mile away.

"It wasn't only because of old customs and reactionary ideas, it was because it really wasn't safe for women to go out and be seen by the landlords and the Kuomintang officers."

There were many more reminiscences of the past, and they all told the same tale of fantastic oppression of the womenfolk by the inhuman customs of feudal society, supported by all the force the Kuomintang rulers could

143

muster. Oppression by the landlords, all the misery of cold and hunger and ignorance, the pains of childbirth under medieval conditions of poverty that doomed countless mothers and children to death or injury. . . . All these passed in review.

Among the most poignant and tragic stories were those of slave-mothers, women who, because of dire need, were forced to live with landlord families to provide them with an heir if the lawful wives were unable to do so. Such were the terrible straits to which the women of the people were driven in Kuomintang times.

"Liberation freed us women from a double yoke," said Tsao Tsai-erh. "It freed us from oppression by the landlords and the idea that men should always be above us. There was a saying here that 'men are always two inches taller than women.' Now all that's been done away with. But we didn't get our freedom all at once. At first, most of us were too timid to take the rights we were given. Only a very few women attended the first mass meetings held after liberation. Most of us continued to live the same old way as before.

"It was really the men who first got the new ideas about women. They attended the meetings where the Communist Party's policy was explained. When the activists came home from these meetings, they urged their wives to 'stand up.' And gradually more women began going to the meetings. But of course there were some selfish die-hards who still tried to keep their womenfolk from asserting their rights.

"The big change came during the movement to overthrow local despots and in the land reform. One woman, Fung Chin-feng, denounced the despot Hu, the 'Old *Pao* Head' at a big meeting of all the households of the village. Hundreds of people were there. Fung Chin-feng became a village cadre along with the men. She visited all the women of the village and explained things to them. Soon

144

we'd got a women's federation started. We elected her chairman. First the women began to attend our own women's meetings to hear the revolutionary policy explained then soon we began attending the general meetings along with the men.

"That's how we came to take an active part in the land reform. We weren't behindhand in showing up the landlords. We took part in the meetings to settle the class status of the villagers and also for distributing the landlords' lands and property.

"We were still backward when it came to field work, though. When the first work-exchange groups were formed we couldn't take much part. We didn't know how to do field work so no one wanted to exchange work with us! It was only when the seasonal mutual-aid team was formed that we had a chance to try our hand. The Party comrades had often said that unless we did productive work in the fields we could never be economically independent. Now the mutual-aid team gave us a chance. The amount of work you did was calculated in points, so even a poor worker could earn a few points to begin with and then get more points as his skill improved. This suited us well.

"Wang Hsueh-yung's wife Ho Hsi-erh was the first to do field work in the seasonal MAT."

I knew her well, Ho Hsi-erh, a buxom country girl strong enough to lift two large baskets of rice weighing well over a hundred catties . . . .

"Tsao Tsai-erh was next!" interrupted the young Youth League member because she knew that Tsai-erh would be modest and not like to put herself forward.

"Weren't you afraid of what people would say?" I asked.

"I knew what some old fogies were saying, but it wasn't so bad because they never said it to my face!"

"They called those two the *Sakapa* of our village!" chimed in Ah Ma. "The *Sakapa* are the national minority people who live in the southeast of the county. Their women work in the fields—they've always done so. That's why the landlords used to say that they ought to worship their ancestors 'under the table.' That meant that they were not civilized human beings and were really nothing but 'sons of bitches!' That's just like the landlords! Insulting good people. Now those *Sakapa* are fine co-op farmers!"

"Well, it was their worry, not mine," continued Tsai-erh. "At first I could only earn three to four points—half a workday — but still that was something. It helped us a lot. Later I could earn six or seven points. Now, when I'm doing work that's within my strength I'm not behind any man.

"Why did I start to do field work? Well, you see, we were a poor-peasant family before the liberation. We lived in a straw hut; we didn't have proper walls to our home. We didn't own a single foot of land. It was only after land reform that we got a proper house to live in, one taken from the landlord. Then my husband joined the People's Volunteers in Korea to help drive out the American invaders. People did all they could to help me and the children but I had to try and help myself too. My husband joined the Youth League and urged me to be progressive too. And the Party comrades like Wang Wen-ken helped me make up my mind and be determined to carry out my decision.

"I worked quite well and since I took a lot of interest in the work of the co-op when it was formed, and had shown myself to be a good worker in the mutual-aid team at weeding and applying fertilizer, they elected me a vice-chairman of the co-op. By this time lots of us women were working in the fields and taking an active part in the co-op work too, so it was only proper that we should have a representative on the management committee.

146

"By this time all the men were as proud as we women were that our co-op had a woman vice-chairman. That shows you how things have changed!

"In the co-op the women have a full say. This has made them eager to study so that they can know all that's going on and speak correctly on all the points that crop up at meetings. I've attended peasant school for half a year now and I'm beginning to read the papers. Nearly all the younger women in the village are attending classes at peasant school.

"And we've a full say too in everything that concerns our homes. Home life is happier."

I asked about the new marriage customs and Ah Ma and the girls were positive that one of the reasons for the happier family life was the fact that now all the young men and women choose their own partners. Men get married now when they are about 24 and the girls when they are about 21. But of course the most important reason is the fact that all the terrible worries about basic human necessities like food and shelter and clothes have ended.

"In the old days there used to be a family row somewhere in the village almost every day. Now there's only one household where they sometimes raise their voices. And that's because the husband is still stubborn. Would you believe it, he really wants his wife to stay at home always and mind the children rather than work for the co-op!"

Everyone joined in vigorously in criticism of the guilty party. Then the talk shifted to ways of ending this "contradiction" between social work and family life and responsibilities and how it could be solved. Finally it was agreed that day nurseries would be an important part of the solution.

By now it was dark. A red candle left over from the New Year festival was lit and in its flickering, homely light we talked of the Soviet Union and Soviet collective farms, of the wonders of farm electrification, electric milking, farm schools and nurseries, mechanical laundries and power stations—the tomorrow of Tumushan.

Mountain Village
in Chingho Township

Chingho —

IV

CHINGHO COLLECTIVE FARM

Up in the Tieh Mu Mountains of Chekiang Province, in January 1955, I met a small peasant brother of the great socialist Anshan Iron and Steel Works.

Here in a valley flanked by lovely mountains covered thickly with scrub and pine, cedar and bamboo groves, over 300 peasant families have formed a socialist collective farm. At that time, it was the first of four in Hsinteng County, of 90 in Chekiang and of several hundreds only in all China. The first such farm had been formed in China in 1950.

They were conscious of the destiny that had linked them with the great socialist industrial giants of New China. They knew they were pioneering a road that would be travelled by more and more of China's peasants in the next few years.

It is a big farm as farms go in China. From end to end its land runs four miles up the valley with arms extending a mile or two up neighbouring valleys with whole mountain peaks of valuable timber in between. Rice and wheat fields, vegetable oil and bean fields cover the valley floor. Thousands of tea bushes dot its fields and hillsides. It owns groves of mulberry and tung oil trees and a growing orchard of choice peaches and pears. It has some 2,000 *mou* of fields and another 10,000 or more *mou* of mountain land.

As I drove in from the county town, lorries were loading thousands of tough, pliable *Tang Cha* boughs to repair and strengthen the dykes at Nanking. In the courtyard of an ancestral temple shaded by ancient trees I saw a row of deep cauldrons for drying tea leaves and a new hand-worked machine for cutting and curling them. This was one of the farm's several processing sheds. At the head of a valley where clear spring water gushes from the mountainside, is a handicraft workshop making fine bamboo paper. It has a series of small reservoirs for rotting the fibres, troughs and presses for making the pulp, and a drying and packing room.

Here and there in the valley are clustered the peasants' houses and cottages. Some are beautifully decorated with traditional black and white designs under the eaves. Here live the farmers, woodsmen, paper makers, tea and silk-worm specialists and huntsmen of this many-sided collective farm. I saw hardy lumberjacks balanced on yoked bamboos shooting the falls on their way down river. Wisps of smoke rose into the blue sky from the fires of charcoal burners. By the side of the highway we passed a tile and brick kiln.

All these, and a school, a cultural centre and meeting rooms are the property and activities of the Chingho Agricultural and Forestry Producers' Collective Farm.

The Chingho Farm is off the beaten track. It lies about eight miles from Hsinteng county town up the valley of the Sung. I was put up comfortably in a spare room above the supply and marketing co-op on the diminutive main street of Hofu Village. This stands in the middle of the farm between the two soaring peaks of Green Mountain and Moon Harmony Mountain.

Looking out of my window I could see the whole street. It seemed pretty poor with its cobble-stones and houses standing much in need of a new coat of whitewash. But

151

delve back five years into its history and it becomes a sort of wonderland.

Before the liberation it was even less of a street. It lay, not beside a broad highway, but by a narrow wheelbarrow track. Two small shops sold sauce and wine, walnuts and rough wheaten cakes. The nearest real shop was over eight miles away in the county town.

In 1950, just before land reform, the supply and marketing co-op opened a branch here. With a staff of two it sold only bare necessities like sauce and salt, for the people were still too poor to buy much more. After land reform it grew. Now that all the peasants are in the collective farm, Hofu has a large general goods store selling all sorts of daily necessities like salt, oil, kerosene for lamps, dried fruits and sweetmeats, crockery and kitchen utensils. It carries a good assortment of cloth, mainly cotton—plain and prints—and also sturdy woollens, socks, galoshes, hats, fountain-pens, electric torches, paper and other stationery, shoes, toothbrushes, soap, face creams; and local products such as umbrellas, sun-hats, straw sandals and baskets of all kinds; farm tools and foodstuffs. These things come in by the lorry load now. In the early days all stock came in on two ends of a carrying pole. The day I arrived I saw a peasant woman buy twenty yards of cloth and clothes for her family. This, I was told, was nothing unusual.

The co-op will take orders for anything a customer needs but is not in stock at the moment. Its warehouses are filled with the products it buys from the peasants: tea, charcoal, bamboos, bamboo shoots, animal skins and so on. Here too is the post-office.

Next door is the school with its gaily singing pupils. The women's federation and the winter school have their classes there too and opposite is the cultural centre with its library and exhibition of pictures on sanitation and care of animals. A few doors up is a carpenters', a barbershop, and a bean-curd merchant; the small fruiterer and cooked-meat shop are attached as agencies to the co-op. The rooms above the co-op are also used by the township administration, so it is a lively centre of village life. And village life today in Hofu is the life of the collective farm.

In the spring of 1951, after the land reform, the peasants of Chingho set up their first mutual-aid teams. Thirteen households in Hofu formed a team for the spring sowing. But it is not so easy to build up a real mutual-aid team. When it threatened to rain, those whose fields had not yet been sown grew restive. Discipline was sorely tried. As harvest time approached, the team actually broke up. Pien Chu-shen, a poor peasant, barely managed to persuade eight of its members to form a new team in time for the harvest.

Pien's father had been a doctor but he died soon after Pien had finished primary school. Then the family had fallen into debt and lost everything. After working on a relative's land for a time, Pien had launched out on his own tilling a few *mou* of rented land. Working hard in the fields, and peddling paper in the off seasons, by the time he was twenty-seven he was able to buy a few *mou* of land and even build a cottage. But again he fell on hard times and when liberation came, though he was an experienced farmer, he owned less than a *mou* of land and, like most of his neighbours, quite a pile of debts.

Land reform gave him and his family two *mou* of fields and two and a half *mou* of mountain land. By good farming he was able in two years to clear off his debts. Always a good neighbour, he was quick to join the mutual-aid team and was a leading spirit in keeping it going.

"But you know, I really still had some capitalist ideas at the back of my mind at that time," he admitted. "I wanted to live in a bigger house and get rich quick. I'd taken an active part in land reform and was village chairman but I'd thought of the mutual-aid team only as a short-cut out of my difficulties. That winter of 1951 I got new ideas. I went as delegate to a district conference. There I heard Comrade Chin, the Party secretary, talk about the two roads before the peasants. One was capitalism: down that road the peasants would scramble against each other as of old; some might get rich, but most would get poorer. The other road was socialism. That way they would organize to get prosperous together.

"This was the first time I'd heard things explained so clearly. I knew then which road we must take. But it needed thinking over to know how we Hofu folk could get on that road. All I could see then was that the first thing was to make our team work well.

"This took up all my thoughts. And then for the first time I heard about collective farms in the Soviet Union. I was so lost in thought those days that sometimes I'd find myself walking past the place I was aiming for, or going to the vegetable oil field instead of the wheat.

"I wasn't the only one thinking like that. These ideas were flying around the countryside. When I came back and told our team members — all poor peasants like myself — about the conference, we all agreed that we must make our team work better.

"Discipline was greatly improved, but we were still stuck with the problem of how to assess our work. Finally we hit on the idea of using the same methods of assessment as farm co-ops in other places used. We were all in high spirits. We set to and reclaimed some wasteland, raised an extra 500 catties of peanuts and many melons, and got bigger yields of rice. The comrades from the district came to help us with the accounting and other difficult jobs. In April 1952 we took in another five households — making eighteen in all — and became a regular farming co-op with pooled land as well as labour. Work was assessed more fairly and accurately in work-points, and paid for out of the common income pool. Owners of land received dividends on their land, which they put into the co-op as shares.

"But don't think things go easily all the time. More members meant more difficulties. There was the extra accounting, extra meetings, and then, you know, we didn't all have the same ideas on things. Some were as keen on co-operation as the best; others were only in for what they could get. Some wanted to rush ahead. Others wanted to crawl.

"Our peasants are practical people. They could see how well the co-op worked by the higher yields it got. After the harvest 35 more households applied to join in a single day. But we had to set a limit at 50 members.

"We worked hard that year. We restored neglected tea gardens, dug more irrigation channels and improved the bamboo groves by cutting away undergrowth to give the fresh shoots a better chance. New members were a bit worried by all this as they thought we'd have done better to spend more time on ordinary field work for current production. But later they saw the sense of this long-term work. The co-op was put to a severe test that year and came through pretty well.

"In other parts of the county co-ops had been formed too hurriedly and there were cases of 'commandism' — rushing the peasants into the co-ops before they fully understood what this meant. The provincial Party committee pointed out that it was essential that the principle of voluntariness be strictly observed and that any peasant who wanted to leave the co-op could do so immediately. In some co-ops more than half the membership left overnight, though they usually went into mutual-aid teams. But by this time we had a good Party organization and strong core of 'activists' here. We mobilized them all to talk to each individual co-op member. We held a general meeting and frankly discussed our achievements and defects, as well as the shortcomings in the work of the committee. When members saw that the success of the co-op depended on

Old cottage: 15 people lived in these four rooms

A former poor peasant's new house

everyone pulling his weight and seeing to it that improvements were made, not a single one left.

"The peasants here were all watching closely to see how the co-ops would make out — there were only three others here in this township — and the way we held firm greatly impressed them. The autumn harvest sent our income up again. We got 430 catties of grain per *mou* as against only 404 the year before, and 366 in 1951 when we were still only a mutual-aid team. Our wheat yield was 88 per cent more than in 1952. And we got 12,000 yuan from co-op side-occupations."

Pien Chu-shen consulted his notebook: "Let's see, the total income of the co-op in 1953 from all sources — farming, forestry and side-occupations — was equivalent to 319,000 catties of grain. The co-op gave every person an average income of 1,110 catties of grain, 55 per cent more than in the previous year. Twenty households increased their incomes from an average of 1,500 catties a head to 2,500. This made such a stir in the township that several mutual-aid teams and another co-op farm merged with us in the early part of 1954 to form a 102 household co-op with 371 members.

"By this time the idea of co-operation had taken firm root among the peasants. The only arguments were about how it should be organized. Some wanted mutual-aid teams and some co-ops. We hadn't thought much about collective farms as yet but the Party Decisions of December 1953 had something to say about them and of course we studied those decisions.

"The general way the co-op was developing, the special advantages of our many-sided economy with our rich bamboo and timber lands, and especially the fact that most of us had a good understanding of the road we were travelling, all seemed to me to point in the direction of a collective. But what tipped the scales in favour of a collective was the battle we waged against floods in 1954.

157

"We never had such floods before! Every river and stream came down in torrents. The bridge over the Sung that has stood more than a score of years was swept away. There were eleven flood crests. We fought every one of them on the 50 *mou* most seriously threatened. The river would break the dyke and sweep everything away leaving silt and stones. We'd dig these away and plant again. Then there'd be another crisis. We saved part of the crop but 20 *mou* was a total loss.

"It was when we cleared away the damage after the third crest that the big discussion began. Some said: 'What's the use of putting so much work on this land? Those who like their landshares will enjoy it while we sweat for it!'

"Many of those who had only small landshares, who depended on work for most of their incomes, wanted to give up this battle against the river and do something more profitable. But the general feeling was that we must fight on and save the crop for the country no matter whose land it was, landshares or no landshares, and discuss things later.

"Despite the flood, we got a good harvest that year. The average yield was 403 catties a *mou*, lower than the year before because of the flood, but side-occupations were better organized and the average income of members rose to 1,162 catties a head, compared to 1,110 in 1953.

"In the discussion that took place after the flood members made it clear that while they were willing and eager to work hard for the common good, they weren't so eager to work in order that 30 per cent of the co-op's income should go to pay dividends on landshares. 'After all,' they argued, 'it's the work that counts. The more work we do, the more we produce for the country. But as long as we have landshares, there'll always be some content to sit back and take it easy!' So more and more members began to want to form a collective farm. In this case landshares would be abolished altogether and payments to members would be based only on labour on the socialist principle of 'to each according to his work!'

"We couldn't make so drastic a change, however, unless every single member agreed.

"There were many discussions. Many worries had to be smoothed away. Those households with many able-bodied members were naturally in favour. Those who had few work hands, hesitated. And so, too, did those who owned rich timber stands or bamboo groves. Some were getting up to 400 yuan every other year from their bamboo groves, with very little labour. At that time mountain lands weren't pooled. You see, when the land reform was carried out we hadn't realized how valuable these mountain tracts were. We calculated the lots very roughly. One *"mou"* of mountain land was really equal in area to several *mou* in the valley fields and the value of the plots varied widely. This gave some peasants greater economic advantages than others and encouraged capitalist ideas among them. That's why even when we organized the co-op farm they weren't eager to pool these lands and share the proceeds as landshares.

"We were able to show such peasants however that though they might lose a little at first, they'd get more in the long run. Centralized management of all the labour and property of the collective farm members would be bound to bring higher yields. We also decided that in the first year, members would get a quarter of all income from their old bamboo groves, with other temporary compensation until their income from work alone was higher than their previous income from all sources.*

---

*Members were also guaranteed 50 per cent of the value of timber cut on their old land in any year within the next five years, and also 10 per cent of the firewood cut on their old land.

"In this way it was finally agreed that four-fifths of the farm income should go to pay labour, and the rest for day-to-day expenditure, reserves and welfare.

"We weren't taking a risky step by any means. Our members were mentally prepared for the change and the farm was economically sound. Members were making twice as much as they did in the mutual-aid teams. We didn't have all our eggs in one basket. Agriculture, forestry and side-occupations each gave us roughly a third of our income. By using new and better methods we were certain to raise yields from 403 to 600 catties a *mou* by 1957. Tea would bring us in 3,500 yuan; bamboos another 1,800; tung oil, silk and other things, like tiles and bricks and paper, bamboo shoots and cartage would bring in large amounts. On the basis of a steady 10 per cent rise in income every year we'll be able by 1957 to give our members an income equivalent to about 2,000 catties of grain a head. (This was an underestimation, for the farm

Building the new school house at Chingho

increased its grain output by 37 per cent in 1955 alone!
— J.C.)

"We've also accumulated quite an amount of common property in the last three years. With five buffaloes and many farm tools it's worth some 2,500 yuan. We have 500 *mou* of land and thousands of *mou* on mountain slopes. In 1953 and '54 we planted 2,000 new tea shrubs, 540 mulberry trees and 2,000 other saplings.

"And what's most important, we've a grand lot of people and a lot of experience in running our farm.

"As a matter of fact, 215 more households soon joined us — good people who had got used to the new ways of doing things in the eight co-ops and mutual-aid teams which merged with us. That brought us a lot of new strength. We formally registered as a collective farm, the first in Hsinteng County, on National Day last year, 1954. At that time in China, there were only a few hundred such collective farms."

If Pien Chu-shen had full confidence in the members, they had no less confidence in him. When I asked a peasant what he thought of the leaders of the co-op, he chuckled as though the question was a naive one. "The district committee's given us a lot of time," he said. "Comrades from the district and county are always on hand to help us. When we were forming the collective farm the county vice-chairman himself came down and stayed to help us. And Chairman Pien is good, good!"

I understood better what he meant when next day there was a fire alarm in the village. I was working when I heard shouts and the scamper of feet running by. I looked out the window. The mild old lady who lived next door was vigorously beating the alarm gong. People were running from all directions to help. A few minutes later as I took a place in the line of villagers handing things from the burning house, I caught a glimpse of Chairman Pien standing astride a straw-roof outhouse, smoke and sparks flying around him, directing the dousing of the roof of the burning house, the breaking of tiles and cutting and throwing off of burning rafters. Soon the fire was under control and put out.

Members today are proud of their farm and its pioneering work.

Farmer Ho Ah-yuan and his family were looking over the new house they were building when I met them. They pointed to the dismal shack they are leaving. It was a vivid contrast. The new house has six large rooms, a fifty-foot frontage, sturdy brick walls, columns and floors of pine and catalpa. It is costing them 500 yuan and is built out of savings and the timber comes from their own land. "We'd never have had this without co-operation!" they said.

Lo Chin-lan has a totally disabled husband and two little boys to care for. She looks after one of the farm's buffaloes, and the welfare fund makes her income up to 75 per cent of the average income of members. The elder boy is at school. "Without the collective farm, I'd have to go out begging!" she said.

Chung Hsueh-chao, 47 years old, is blind. He told me: "The people's government has freed me from the agricultural tax. The collective farm gives me the kind of work I can do and makes up with a subsidy what else I need to keep my family. It's given me a 15 yuan advance on wages already this year."

With six in the family, and he the only breadwinner, a two month bout of sickness would have spelt catastrophe for Tsu Tien-pao in the old days. He was the first member to fall sick when the collective farm was formed. He received a subsidy from its welfare fund of 200 catties of grain. "That was real help," he says gratefully. "I'd been an active member of the co-op farm but I never dreamt I'd belong to a big collective farm with such big reserves it can give members sickness benefits! That's socialism!"

162

The sick benefit is automatically paid at the rate of half a workday for 30 days. Anyone injured doing farm work gets free medical treatment and receives a benefit of half a workday for a period calculated on the average of his previous earnings.

He introduced me to his twins born last year. "I call them Double Silver and Double Gold for prosperity!"

A few doors away I met the first baby and mother to receive the farm's maternity benefit. Little Tse-kung's mother said: "The baby came in August and I stopped work in July. But before that the farm committee arranged for me to do specially light work and when I needed it I could take a rest without worrying!" She got the equivalent of 20 workdays for the time she was at home before and after the baby came. The general rule is that no member of the farm in good standing should have an income worth less than 500 catties a year a head. This covers basic needs in food.

Those families with many work hands are very well satisfied. Pien Yung-ling is one of these. Strong and healthy himself, he has two grown sons and a family of six. In 1953 he earned 5,400 catties of grain from labour and landshares. In 1954, in the collective farm, he earned over 8,000 catties in payment for labour alone.

He has repaired and enlarged his house, bought quilts and new clothes for the family, and farm tools and fertilizer for his personal allotment. "There's several of us working and there's work and to spare in the collective. Our big farm has rich mountains and we've made the land fertile. All we've got to do now is to raise output — and that means work. I'm satisfied. I sold a thousand catties of rice to the state last year and I was glad to be able to do so. I'll sell more this year. All our people must have enough to eat!

"In the old days we Chingho people were the poorest of the poor in this county. Prosperity was always just around the corner for us but we're catching up on it fast now!"

Ho Pu-yuen was one of those who hesitated to join at first. He was for the collective farm, but his wife was very vocally against. The previous year their income had been worth 7,000 catties of grain and quite a bit of this was from their valuable bamboo grove. In the first year, if they joined the collective, he calculated they'd get 6,600 catties income for their work, but would get nothing from the bamboo grove if it were pooled without compensation. The committee then explained that they'd get 30 yuan as compensation, but this still wouldn't make their income up to what they'd got the previous year. The argument in the house was heated. Their son, a Youth League member, sided with his father. Finally his wife was won over.

He told her: "The people gave me those bamboos in the first place anyway. If we work hard we'll get more in the collective than they're worth. Outside the collective what would we have? Some bamboos and we'd lose our self-respect, waiting for others to make the collective farm a success before we join. I'll not leave it to others to do the spade work for me. That's no way to prosperity!"

Eight months after it was founded, although it had not yet cropped its first harvest, the Chingho Collective Farm stood firm. It was the fulcrum of life in the township, 74 per cent of whose population were now working in it. It had a labour force of 712 men and women; valuable common property including 56 buffaloes and many implements. It had already drawn up its plan of labour: 18,000 workdays in the fields; 20,000 for capital construction: building houses, digging ponds, raising dykes, improving fields; 22,000 on side-occupations (paid for at piece rates); 14,000 on industrial crops and a reserve in hand of 18,000 workdays.

It had already reclaimed 350 *mou* of wasteland, and cleared 225 *mou* of old tea gardens. It will clear another 560 *mou* of hillside for sowing maize (this to raise more pigs), and more tea. Its tea is famous. In the old days unscrupulous merchants used to repack it and sell it as *Lung Ching*, the best tea in China. It will plant 3,000 tung oil and 300 tea oil trees, and 500 mulberry trees. It will cut 150,000 green bamboos this year, 15 per cent more than last year. It will make 6,000 blocks of paper worth 9,600 yuan and make 1,200 yuan worth of tiles.

It has signed a link contract with the supply and marketing co-op which states that "in order to fulfil the national production plan for 1955, to raise more grain, support the industrialization of the country, further the struggle to liberate Taiwan and steadily improve the livelihood of the peasants," it will sell the co-op 23,000 catties of pork, 25,000 catties of tea, 300,000 catties of charcoal, 60,000 catties of succulent bamboo shoots and other products and receive in return the fertilizers needed to introduce double cropping on more than half its rice lands.

The total value of its agricultural products will be some 48,600 yuan. Side-occupations will bring its income up to 138,600 yuan.

The peasant book-keepers of the Chingho Collective Farm are dealing familiarly in figures that a few years ago would have seemed astronomical.

My last impression as I left Chingho was perhaps the most vivid of my stay.

Just below the village a small hill rises out of the valley floor. The cultivated fields reach to its base, but it is thickly covered with tough scrub; a small wilderness in the midst of order. Now a red Youth League flag was planted on its summit. Fire and smoke enveloped one side. A brigade of Youth League members, wielding hoes, sickles and axes with all the determination of the People's Liberation Army storming an enemy fortress, was advancing up its sides. A wide, cleared swathe was left in its wake. On the newly upturned soil girls were already planting saplings of precious teak.

Clearing
Virgin Soil—

V

CHENGLING DISTRICT

HOW LIFE CHANGES

In January 1955 Chengling Rural District (*chu*) was one of the four making up Hsinteng County.* It now had 30,000 *mou* of arable land: 25,000 irrigated and 5,000 dry, and over 5,260 *mou* of forest lands. It had over 4,300 peasant households with a total agricultural population of around 16,000 souls. The average share of land per person was 1.6 *mou*.

The district centre itself was located in Sunghsi hamlet, one of the larger of the 226 hamlets or natural villages in the district. These are grouped for minor administrative matters into 32 villages (*chun*) and these in turn into eight townships (*hsiang*) which have their own elected people's congress, the basic organ of the people's democratic power in China, and people's council, which the congress elects to form the local government authority. This sees to the smooth running of public services and performs all the normal functions of local government. Local government greatly improved after the general election in 1954.

The hamlets and villages have branches of the various people's organizations such as the women's federation, the

---

*At the end of 1955, as will be described later, the district was abolished. The natural bounds of new co-op farms overflowed the old administrative boundaries.

Youth League and peasants' association, but these mostly had their basic organizations at the hamlet level in the co-op farms. Some co-ops already included whole hamlets or several villages or, as at Chingho, even a whole township. The district centre was an important link in the administrative system. It stood midway between the township people's government and the Hsinteng County (*hsien*) administration made up of the county people's congress and council, which in turn comes directly beneath the provincial people's congress. (See chart on page 19.)

The district itself had no congress or council but it was the centre of activities organized by all the eight townships of Chengling District through their district office. The district office had a staff of three: a director, accountant and secretary. The various townships could, of course, refer directly to the county administration, or to the province or Peking for that matter, but two-way contacts normally ran through the district office.

So far as the Communist Party is concerned, wherever there are enough members (a minimum of three), a basic Party group can be formed. Many such had already been formed in mutual-aid teams or co-ops. But there were still relatively few Party members in Chengling District, so here the basic centres of Party activity were the township branches, with sub-branches in the large mutual-aid teams and co-ops. Today, throughout China, there are Party branches in nearly all townships. Their work is to give day-to-day leadership to the co-op movement and other tasks set by the Party and make full use of the joint co-op organizations or "networks" established around all the important co-ops. They work hard to make their townships models in the co-op movement.

The district Party committee was made up of a secretary, an organizer, delegates from the various township branches, some full-time propaganda workers and a comrade to direct work among the women. It concentrated its main attention on the co-op movement, co-ordinated the work of the various township branches and, in its turn, passed down directives from the county Party committee and informed the higher Party organizations of the progress of work in the townships. These reports were gathered not only at the fortnightly meetings of township Party branch secretaries, but in the course of work in Sungyen Township, the key township of the district, and in the key co-op, the Hsinyen Co-op.

The Hsinteng county committee leads the work in all parts of the county, checks up on fulfilment of Party policy and directives, collects reports from its subordinate organizations and townships and analyses and sums up this experience for the general guidance of work in the county. Just as the district Party committee had a key township and two key units of the co-op movement under its special care for work and study, so the county committee has a key district and key township and several key co-ops and mutual-aid teams under its special charge.

In the early days the Party organization had functioned chiefly through its committees in the peasants' associations. The county chairman of the peasants' association was here concurrently the secretary of the county Party committee. It was the peasants' association that was the main hive of political activity in getting the co-op movement started with work-exchange groups and seasonal mutual-aid teams. Later the organizational structure of civil administration was perfected in the rural areas. Revolutionary military rule gave way to popularly elected civil administrations. The work of governing became more complex and specialized, the Party organization, however, was stronger and more numerous and so the county Party committee in 1952 set up its rural work department and then, in 1953, established its agricultural production section of the department for mutual aid and co-operation, which takes special care of the agricultural co-operative movement. It is the special responsibility of the Party organization at all levels to train cadres for the co-op movement.

Chengling District as the key district of the county had the first co-ops in the county. Most of its townships had famous co-ops. In Sungyen Township there was the Hsu Kuei-yung Co-op, the first in the county; Yungho Township (the key township of the county) had the Yang Yu-chuan Co-op, in 1953 one of the best rice-growers in the county; Szeho Township had the Wang Wen-ken Agricultural Co-operative and Chingho Township the Pien Chu-shen Collective Farm which in 1955 was the first of four in the county of this higher type of co-op—a socialist collective farm, a model of its kind and a most important centre for gaining experience for what would be the next step in the movement.

All these levels of administration: township, district and county, have their attention concentrated on the co-op movement as the main lever for the advance of the peasants and all the county's people to prosperity. It is the job of the district centre to see that the health service, the educational institutions, the People's Bank, and all the many other organizations serving the people, function well and function in the service of the co-op movement. The supply and marketing co-ops and handicraft co-ops coordinate their activities through their county federation of co-operatives. This in turn is affiliated to the provincial, and All-China Federation of Co-operatives.

By January 1955, over 90 per cent of the whole rural population eligible to join had entered the 25 mutual-aid teams and 84 co-op farms of the district. This was 84 per cent of the entire rural population (including rich peasants and former landlords, and others as yet ineligible to join).

This was the solid social foundation on which was founded the steady increase in agricultural output in the district and the growing prosperity of its people. The output of rice rose from 7,640,000 catties in 1949 with a yield of 300 catties per *mou* to a record of 10,950,000 catties in 1952 with a yield of 430 catties per *mou*. In 1953 and 1954 output was 10,560,000 catties and 10,340,000 catties respectively. It was only thanks to the tenacity and spirit of the co-op movement that such yields were achieved. There were exceptional conditions of drought and flood in these two years. Everyone agreed that such weather conditions in Kuomintang times would have led inevitably to widespread distress and temporary famine.

In 1955, with a wealth of experience behind them and with the launching of the new methods of cultivation of double crops and late maturing high yield seed, the co-operative farmers of Chengling District were eagerly looking forward to record harvests with yields of between 500 and 550 catties a *mou*.

Sunghsi hamlet, which was host to the district centre, boasts of only a single short lane that can be walked in five slow minutes. But in business hours it is rarely empty. Here were the new government and Party offices, the tax office and state wine and cigarette wholesale office, the big supply and marketing co-operative, which this spring remodelled and enlarged its premises to take in a frontage of some fifty feet, and a couple of smaller agencies selling fruit, meat and other foods, several small shops and stalls, the People's Bank, the credit co-operative, a couple of sewing co-operatives, a machine-powered mill, a basket-making co-operative, and a wizened old folk artist who makes lovely paper lanterns and paper cuts for festivals and fries sweet rice cakes for the everyday nourishment of sweet-toothed inhabitants and visitors. Then there is the open air theatre and meeting place and the cultural centre with its classrooms for the peasant school, reading room and library.

Down a quiet side street facing the mill-race is the health department's spotlessly clean courtyard with its clinic and dispensary attached. This, like so many other public institutions, is housed in a former landlord's dwelling. Intricately carved beams support its upper story of aged redwood.

Chengling District is fair under the beaming sun of early spring. Dawn comes at six o'clock. And soon the farmers, after an early breakfast of rice gruel and pickled vegetables and tea, are in the fields or at their paper-making troughs for their day's work. At lunch time and in the still evenings smoke from the wood fires comes from every cottage in the valley as the main meals of the day are prepared. This in itself is a sign of the times. In Chengling District no one goes hungry these days.

Then comes the sunset that brings out all the latent colour in the hills. In the warm damp air—for there is a deal of rain in Chekiang at this time—the sun often sinks in a truly tropic splendour of colour, of shell pinks, blazing red purples and emerald greens which throw the surrounding mountains into sharp lined silhouettes of rock and tree.

Though the days may be so hot that the farmers shed their coats and even vests, the nights still have a touch of winter cold. And Chekiang winters are as cold as the summers are hot. But the peasants are hardy folk. There are no fireplaces in the houses. But only the old folk seek the warmth of the cooking ranges. When it gets unpleasantly cold the people carry their little wicker baskets with shallow tin trays inside into which they shovel a few handfuls of warm ashes and charcoal. Carrying this by the handle, they keep both hands warm. Old ladies carry them comfortably under their aprons. Most baskets have a wire mesh covering the ashes. You can take your shoes off if your feet are cold and warm them by baking them gently over the embers.

Paddy fields are mirrors of sky and mountains and villages. Rape seed, grown for its oil, blossoms in early spring with a bright yellow flower. Spring wheat makes

172

bright touches of green in the dun-brown fields even in January. Tea shrubs, bamboos, holly, and in the hill farms, cedar and pine and other evergreens contrast their leafy masses with the bare, contorted limbs of the mulberries.

A fine, broad stream, the Sung Creek, runs through the district from northeast to southwest. It has been dammed at intervals and this keeps water flowing at a depth as long as there is any flow from the hills at all. It brings irrigation to the farmers' fields, power to many water-wheels, water for paper-making and other crafts, and for the peasant households. It forms picturesque reaches where the children love to play. It swirls in a broad pool around the former temple theatre which is now a popular club near the district centre. Too shallow for boats, bamboo rafts are poled on it by watermen taking timber, bamboo and other produce down from the hill villages.

Chekiang houses are sturdy affairs. The poor peasants live in one- or two-storied houses which they build themselves of sun-dried bricks or stone. There was good building timber in the mountains surrounding the valley (there still is today around the mountain villages) and with luck even some poor peasants in the old days managed to build an upper storey with a wood floor. The mud huts and thatched hovels of the poorest peasants have long since disappeared or been turned to other uses. The former poor peasants and landless labourers who lived in them now share the landlord mansions.

The landlords built roomy two-storied houses of stone and wood plastered all over in white or grey and shaped like fortresses, squat and square with few windows on the outside and the rooms looking onto an inside courtyard. Others are of more attractive form and decorated by folk craftsmen in an altogether characteristic local style with black and white geometrical designs of considerable interest and often of great beauty.

173

The whole valley is dotted with these big white walled buildings buttressed by clay and wattle outhouses and stables and with an inevitable clump of shade trees nearby.

The houses of the old middle and rich peasants hover between these two extremes.

The new government offices are built on pleasing, matter-of-fact lines, economical and functional, of grey brick, with red tiles, somewhat in the style of garden villages in England.

Many peasants are now building new houses or enlarging or repairing their old ones. Craftsmen and decorative artists are in big demand. The collective farmers favour the style of dwelling that used to be built by well-to-do farmers of old. This is a two-storied affair with three stout stone walls and the front of timber with a wide ground floor veranda and a recessed upper row of windows. My drawing of a new house in the Chingho Collective Farm, belonging to the chairman's brother, is a good example of this type of house.

In Chengling District the peasants made a fresh start in life with the liberation and the land reform. Now the promise of those days has turned into solid reality. They already enjoy the beginnings of a prosperity and cultural well-being that hearten them for further advance.

The beauty of the countryside is no longer a rebuke to the inhumanity, dirt, ignorance and abject poverty of the old days. Now the peasants are well clothed. But they are thrifty and throw nothing away that can still be used as decent working clothes. On festivals and holidays they are as well dressed as the average workaday city crowds. Poor peasants wore only rope sandals in the old days. In wet weather, summer or biting winter, they sloshed through the mud in bare feet. Today the average family is well shod in black cotton Chinese slippers for good wear (padded in winter), straw sandals for rough wear or galoshes in the wet. Leather boots, raincoats, umbrellas are no longer uncommon. Every bed has a warm blanket or quilt. There are some few luxuries like thermos bottles or oil lamps with modern wicks and glass chimneys in most houses. They wash with scented soap, have good pottery or enamelled hand-basins and are sanitation conscious. The old festering sores and underfed looks among the children have long since disappeared. They are small but wiry and full of high spirits.

This is mainly the result of better feeding, but the district health centre has done wonders with practical work and propaganda. In many houses animals used to be crowded into the rooms along with people and the night soil buckets to be safe from thieves. A rich aroma pervaded the peasants' hovels. All that has ended.

Lice, scabies, kala-azar, malaria, dysentery were rampant. Today vermin have been wiped out and these diseases too have been or are being wiped out, but intestinal worms are still a problem.

The clinic works on the principle that "prevention is better than cure." It has encouraged the peasants to stable their animals properly — and this incidentally makes for more manure — build proper latrines, clean up garbage dumps and turn garbage into compost. In Sungyen Township the women made nearly 400 compost heaps in 1954 and presented the co-ops with 60,000 catties of first-rate fertilizer. In such ways the clinic helps production directly. It runs regular "clean up" emulation drives with banners and prizes for the best teams and co-ops. Dr. Pan, head of the health centre, complains that there was a bit of backsliding last year compared to 1953, but there is a vast difference between sanitation today and two years ago. It is beyond comparison with pre-liberation times.

A campaign of inoculations is being systematically carried out to encompass the entire district population. Vaccination teams go out every spring and autumn. Each person vaccinated now has his record kept. In 1953 and 1954 inoculations were given in all the villages along the main highway for cholera, typhus and diphtheria. A big and successful drive has been made against malaria in the hill villages where mosquitoes breed rapidly in the bamboo groves. In the Pien Chu-shen Collective Farm atabrine injections were given to each member, mosquito breeding grounds were cleaned up, and the peasants were urged to buy mosquito nets, which they can now afford. And there have been no epidemics since then.

Greater cleanliness and worm powders have had a good effect in reducing this scourge of the children. When the first test was made in the district primary school 105 out of 120 children were found to be suffering from worms.

The fight against quack remedies, that were peddled by unscrupulous charlatans or had general currency due to ignorance, has been won.

The clinic has two Western-trained doctors, one male nurse, two nursing assistants, a pharmacist. Its seven Chinese doctors trained in traditional medical practice are very popular among the peasants. Their two mobile teams in 1953 treated 3,425 patients and 2,475 in 1954. In 1953 and again in 1954 the clinic gave 3,250 smallpox and 2,500 cholera and typhus injections.

Particular attention has been paid to mother and child welfare. The clinic now has 19 newly trained midwives using modern methods of childbirth. Sixty-year-old Chen Ah-fan, who before liberation saw 30 per cent of the babies she delivered annually die, has been retrained. Last year she delivered 172 babies every one of which is alive today. Now nearly every expectant mother gets pre-natal check-ups. It is nothing unusual for engaged couples to get medical check-ups before marriage.

The new generation in Chengling District is growing up with a knowledge of modern methods of hygiene and sanitation. This is the assurance of a healthy, strong collective farm generation for tomorrow.

Two big mass organizations centred in the district have a close and important bearing on the new life of the peasants: the supply and marketing co-operative and the credit co-operative networks.

The supply and marketing co-op was launched in 1949 just a few months after liberation with a share capital of 1,000 yuan. In 1953, when the General Line of the Party was announced and the peasants responded to the slogan "Wipe out the second root of poverty—middleman exploitation!" (the landlord yoke is the first root), share capital increased to 8,000 yuan. By 1955, it was 40,000 yuan all held by poor and middle peasants. In 1956 it increased again.

In addition to its shops for consumer goods, the supply and marketing co-op gives its peasant clients and owners good value for the farm supplies of every kind which it stocks. It also acts as their agent in selling the products of their side-occupations: paper, bamboo goods, bamboo shoots, tea, pigs, and so on.

If the supply and marketing co-op among its other benefits forced the private merchant to toe the line with fair prices and good quality for customers, the credit co-ops and the People's Bank have put paid to usury in the district.

Usury was one of the "knives" which stuck in the peasants' backs. A debt of sometimes only a few catties of grain at compound interest was often the start of ruin, starvation and death for a poor peasant family. Debts to landlords were wiped out by the land reform, but debts between neighbours or friends still had to be repaid. It took two or even more years after land reform to repay some of these debts. And even after the land reform there were not a few capitalistically minded rich peasants and some backward well-to-do middle peasants who took advantage of the situation to advance new usurious loans to peasants in difficulties. Cases of usurious loans contracted between members of mutual-aid teams or co-op farms were not unusual even in 1953. It must be remembered that at that time the People's Bank could not possibly attend to every call on it nor could the reserve funds controlled by the committees of teams or co-ops. In the beginning of 1954 a number of small credit groups were formed in several teams and co-ops. The first was actually formed in Pien Chu-shen's collective farm. By June that year thirty had been formed in five townships and on this basis the credit co-op organization of the district was founded. Seven townships have one credit co-op each; and the eighth has a credit department (an intermediate form of credit co-op between a group and full co-op). This made Cheng-ling District, as it proudly calls itself, "a credit co-op district."

By giving prompt assistance to those in temporary need, these co-ops have removed a fertile source of misunderstanding between neighbours and between the poor and middle peasants in the mutual-aid teams and co-ops. They help to put idle savings to productive use and enable the People's Bank to concentrate on its main job of solving the big financial difficulties and needs of the co-operative movement. This has helped to consolidate the co-operative movement in general.

When the credit co-ops totted up their accounts at the end of 1954 they showed that nearly 75 per cent of all the households in the district were now members; that the peasants had put in savings totalling 37,450 yuan and received loans totalling 32,440 yuan. Interest rates are low. They vary from 0.75 per cent on a loan designed to increase production (to buy a buffalo or material for a side-occupation) to 1.5 per cent on a "living expenses loan" to repair the house or celebrate a wedding.

Back of the credit co-ops stands the People's Bank. They had, in fact, received substantial loans from the bank. The bank is another bulwark of the co-operative movement since it was established in the district in 1951 and began its work of mobilizing the peasants' savings, providing insurance policies and loans to aid the peasants in solving day-to-day problems and financing large-scale projects in the teams and co-ops. In 1953, it gave the peasants loans totalling nearly 40,000 yuan. The next year it advanced 1,150 yuan to co-op farms, and 21,200 yuan to mutual-aid teams. A large part of these loans were used to buy fertilizer, "the key to bigger production."

Always a hard working, diligent people, the inhabitants of Chengling District have gained in stature as a result of the confidence which inspires them as emancipated, land-owning farmers and successful co-operators. They have indeed "stood up." They have in short order rid themselves of those bad habits that were the product of the old life of worry and privation.

Gambling has totally disappeared. In the old days it was a scourge of the district. You'll have to go a long way to find a drunk these days. The comrades at the district office knew of only one. He lives in Hsiho Township. "He's an old drunk from before the liberation. His family has a lot of manpower and he takes advantage of it!" they said sorrowfully.

Thieving? Well, the worst thieves—the landlords—are either being reformed through labour—behind bars, if their thievery was combined with other crimes, or in their own fields. The small thieves, who were their hangers-on, have been won back to an honest life. A high level of honesty is not only expected but given by civil servants or elected people's deputies in official positions. Fighting and brawling are things of the past. The big tyrants and their hireling bullies have been dealt with long ago. There are few family squabbles and fights, and these are mostly dealt with by the team or co-op members themselves with the assistance of the women's federation or Youth League or other appropriate mass organization.

Family life is happier. Why shouldn't it be? The publication of the Marriage Law ended forced marriages; women who suffered from tyrannical, old-fashioned husbands were emancipated and, if need be, freed. Today all marriages are from free choice, otherwise they will not be registered by the people's government and they will not be countenanced by the awakened public opinion of the teams and co-op farms.

I close these notes on one of the most charming pictures I saw in Chengling District: a young bride coming down a narrow trail from a mountain village. No road or animals here to draw a bridal carriage and somehow the bride and her trousseau had to be conveyed to her new home! So the young bridegroom had come to fetch her with his sturdy wheelbarrow. The bride on one side and her new boxes tied to the other side with crimson sashes. And the bridegroom smiling as he pushed his charming load home, down by the stream, over the old bridge by the flowering plum blossom and nodding bamboos.

In the Mountains—

PEASANT THEATRE

A bright light shone over the pink and white building that stands where the Sung Creek cuts the main road from Hangchow to Hsinteng county town. The crash of drums and cymbals announcing that the play was about to start could be heard from more than two *li* away. From every direction, bright dots in the darkness, swinging lanterns and flickering torchlights converged on this source of light and sound. Groups of peasants wended their way in single file over the narrow paths between the paddy fields to this central point in the valley. From far away you could hear the excited chatter of hundreds of voices.

In the old days, this was a temple. It still is, but no one worships the field gods here any more. Over the doors are religious inscriptions easy to read but hard to understand. One says: "The Tiger Roars." But no one hereabouts knows what this refers to. On the wall nearby, slogans have been painted in red characters: "Mao Tse-tung is our guide!" and "Liberate Taiwan!"

This was and is also a theatre. It has a large stage used for the performance of religious and secular plays. Before liberation it was used only as a meeting place when the landlords or Kuomintang officials summoned the people together to hear about some new order or exaction. Sometimes a travelling commercial theatrical troupe put on a show here.

After liberation it was repaired and, by unanimous decision of the peasants, school rooms were built inside it and the stage and auditorium cleaned up. It is now the main local civic centre of the nearby villages. Here are the overflow classrooms of the school next door and rooms for the peasants' literary classes. The auditorium is used for public meetings, cinema shows and theatrical performances by local and other troupes.

When we arrived it was already filled to overflowing. Stalls set up at the entrance were selling sugar-cane, rice cakes and other sweetmeats and *hun tun* meat broth with tiny meat-filled dumplings. They were doing a lively trade. Children had clambered up to vantage points on the window-sills and even onto the stage. Seating accommodation is limited still, so many brought their own benches and stools, but many would stand untiringly through the whole performance which lasted from seven-thirty to past eleven.

White letters on the maroon coloured curtain announced the name of the troupe: "Theatrical Troupe of Shuihan Village." This is a joint troupe formed by several farm co-operatives of the district, one of some 8,000 amateur troupes in the province of Chekiang, and they were presenting an opera entitled *Wu Sung Kills the Tiger.* This is an adaptation of one of the most famous episodes in *Shui Hu Chuan,** the great 14th century novel that relates the adventures of a hundred and eight heroes of the people who revolted against imperial oppression and injustice.

Everyone knows this story by heart, but there was a special interest in the night's performance, because the troupe was going to present a revised version of it written since the liberation. Furthermore it would be in the *Yueh Chu* form of Shaohsing opera which is particularly popular among the peasants here.

Yueh Chu is a local operatic form that originated some forty years ago in Shaohsing County of Chekiang. This is only a few score miles southeast of Hsinteng County. It began when the old peasant ballads, based on local folk tales and life, evolved into duets with drum and castanet

---

*Translated as *All Men Are Brothers* or *Water Margin.*

184

accompaniment, and then, with added dialogue and airs played on the flute or *hu chin* violin, developed into opera.

At the time of liberation this Shaohsing opera had a fairly rich repertoire. One of its characteristics was that in its stage form it was adapted for plays in which all roles are played by actresses. When it first came to the towns and was taken up by professional theatres, it was acted by both actors and actresses. Later, as it was adapted to the sentimental taste of the men and women of the idle rich among the petty-bourgeois merchant families who frequented the tea-shop theatres, it turned more and more to romantic love themes. Following the fashion set by one particularly popular troupe, actresses gradually took over all the roles.

Two types of Shaohsing opera emerged. The Shaohsing *Ta Pan* represents the stricter form of traditional opera with very set forms of music, singing and arrangement of dialogue. But this convention has not found great favour among the peasants. They prefer the somewhat freer form of *Yueh Chu* which has evolved with a wider range of themes and treatment and which, while having all women troupes, also permits both men and women to act together.

This form of Shaohsing opera has become very popular throughout Chekiang and Kiangsu. The peasants particularly love the romantic operas *Liang Shan-po and Chu Ying-tai* (The Butterfly Lovers), *The White Snake* and *The Western Chamber* in this style.

Several outstanding artists, among them the brilliant actress Yuan Hsueh-fen and her all-women-troupe (whose film version of *The Butterfly Lovers* is now known all over China and in many countries abroad), have done a great deal to bring a new progressive spirit back into Shaohsing opera and rid it of the feudal and philistine banalities and false sentimentalism it picked up in the Kuomintang cities. The authentic character of *The Butterfly Lovers* and *The White Snake* as stories of true love frustrated by the evil forces and prejudices of feudal society, is now brought out more vividly. Peasant audiences see them today with renewed interest because they too have waged and are waging a struggle for marriages based on mutual love and respect and against the arranged marriages and prejudices of the past.

The new cultural groups and theatrical troupes of Chekiang have been able to take the more flexible *Yueh Chu* form of Shaohsing opera, not so firmly wedded to tradition as the *Ta Pan*, and adapt it even to modern themes. The amateur Shaohsing troupes, of which there are some 200 in Chekiang alone in peasants' co-ops, workers and students' clubs and other institutions, also play a vital part in this rebirth of Shaohsing opera. Thus many of the old operas have been revised in the light of modern ways of thinking. Some lively controversies have developed around some of them. Lovers of the classics all, bold innovators, timid conservatives, and even "fence-sitters" battle over "what is permissible," and "where the line should be drawn."

Wu Sung Kills the Tiger is one of these storm points. It is something of a novelty too in *Yueh Chu* form as the hero is a virile fighting man acted by an actor and the Hsinteng audience was anxious to see it in its new version.

It should be explained at once that opera-goers in this part of the county are still divided roughly into those who go to *see* opera and those who go to hear as well as see it. And at the start of the proceedings the upper hand was definitely held by those who came to see. These worthies thought they already knew what was going to happen and what was going to be said and sung since they had heard this story told many times before. Thus it was that when the children had been cleared from the stage and the play began, frantic handwaving for silence, inaudible appeals from the producer in the wings, loud "shushing" from the camp of "hearers" and, finally, piercing blasts on a whistle by the manager, failed to still the gay chatter and comment. Even the strident music was drowned. The actors went on doggedly. They might just as well have been acting a wordless pantomime for all that could be heard.

This attitude to opera was of course no new thing. It was a hangover from the past. It was quite usual in the old tea-house theatres where idle patrons often came just to while away the time and drank tea, ate cakes and gossiped throughout the performance.

Then suddenly the general hubbub dissolved into isolated pools of talk. By the second act one could distinctly hear the actors' words. The see-ers as well as hearers in the audience had grasped that this was something different they were looking at. Pan Ching-lien, the heroine, was different from of old. She was not that heartless hussy and coquette we had always thought her! From that moment, all that took place on the stage was watched and listened to with intense interest.

This temple theatre, like most of the traditional theatres which stand in almost every sizable Chinese village, is something like the Elizabethan theatre of England. The stage itself is covered by a lovely roof with soaring ends supported on four large columns. It stands a good six feet above the floor of the hall. Beautiful and intricate carvings decorate the crossbeams. The well of the auditorium, about forty feet square, where the stalls would be in the usual enclosed theatre, is an open space, open to the sky. Wide covered verandas flank this space to left and right and a deep covered area extends about sixty feet to the rear wall of the auditorium. Here the spectators are well protected from the weather. But those in the open well of the theatre, though they have the best view of the stage, are shelterless. And now it began to rain.

Numerous umbrellas appeared; those who had come fore-armed in galoshes and raincoats squatted imperturbably in their places. The rest, improvident, after a stubborn holding of their coveted places directly in front of

187

the stage, were forced to drift back under shelter as the rain fell more heavily.

But the play went on. No one took any more notice of the rain than it actually deserved, and by now all available attention was riveted on the stage.

Wu Sung, a burly peasant, was well played. He is a rough-hewn character with a heart of gold. He quaffs a hogshead of wine and goes drunk into the forest. Twirling his metal staff with acrobatic skill and to the immense delight of the small boys in the audience, he meets and swiftly disposes of the tiger. He is duly rewarded by the local magistrate and made a commander of troops.

Yueh Chu production techniques make use of many of the conventions of the classical Peking opera. There is the same opening and closing of unseen doors and the riding of a horse indicated by the flourishing of a tasselled whip. Many of the hand and arm movements too are adapted from this great source. But these conventions are integrated with a more naturalistic style of movement. Song is interwoven with recitative and ordinary spoken dialogue. There is a bare minimum of scenery — a great convenience to the peasant theatres. So while Wu Sung came into the inn through a real door, he staggered out through a make-believe one. The forest he went into was made up of a prop-man holding a couple of boughs of real evergreen from the nearby mountains and a cloth draped over two chairs to represent a rock. As in Peking opera, our imaginations made up the rest of the scenery.

But, back to the play. It so happens that Wu Sung's brother, a pastry cook, is living in that same town. He has just married a beautiful girl, Pan Ching-lien. It was an arranged marriage and she married him against her will. He is a rather stupid fellow and he tries to show off before her by boasting of Wu Sung's prowess even though this means emphasizing his own weakness and silliness. He asks Wu Sung to live in his house. Wu Sung, however,

an honourable man, seeing the dangers of introducing himself into such a household, leaves abruptly to lodge elsewhere.

All this was much as in the original tale. But then the
stage version developed along its own lines. In the original
story Pan Ching-lien loathes her misshapen husband and
tries to make love to Wu Sung. When she fails to attract
him she starts an affair through a grasping go-between
with a dissolute rich scoundrel named Hsimen Ching. Her
husband hears of this and threatens to tell Wu Sung. To
save themselves, the guilty three poison him with arsenic.
Wu Sung however learns of the crime and takes summary
vengeance by disposing of the lover, and the two guilty
women. He is then forced to flee and joins the other
heroes of the *Shui Hu Chuan.*

But tonight we see that Pan Ching-lien is no sinner but
deeply sinned against. She is a victim of the feudal marriage system. But despite this she is a faithful wife. She
repulses the advances of Hsimen Ching but he seduces
her with the connivance of the go-between. Returning
home she tells her husband of the crime committed against
her, but before he can inform Wu Sung, Hsimen Ching
and the go-between arrive to "arrange matters." This
they do by giving him poisoned wine. He dies in agony.

Wu Sung however learns of the crime. He asks the
magistrate to punish the guilty; but the magistrate is himself in the pay of the powerful Hsimen Ching and gives
Wu Sung a flogging for his presumption.

Wu Sung then takes justice into his own hands. He
kills the seducer in a fierce duel and disposes of the callous
go-between. Then he comes to the bier of his brother to
announce that retribution is complete. The unfortunate
Pan Ching-lien in a fit of shame and utter remorse for the
tragedy of which she is the innocent cause, commits sui-
cide. She is mourned by Wu Sung and all around.

I remembered hearing criticism of this play among some earnest but rather prim intellectuals; they objected that it was a "distortion of the classics," but as I looked around me I couldn't help feeling that the criticism seemed irrelevant. There was no doubt how close this story was to the lives of the people here. There were women here who had been seized by landlord bullies in the past. There were men here who, only a few years ago, had seen their womenfolk carried off by powerful landlords, shielded by corrupt Kuomintang magistrates. And how they had longed then for a Wu Sung to avenge them!

And finally a "Wu Sung" had come and "killed the tiger" — and was there now to protect them!

The rain had stopped. The clouds had blown away. As we walked homewards in the deep, star-studded night, from somewhere above we heard the drone of a plane. The People's Liberation Army was, as always, awake.

Processing Tea

THE DISTRICT SECRETARY

Hsinyen is a place favoured by nature. It is the sort of place that when you come upon it suddenly, you involuntarily say to yourself: "I could be happy here!" It stands just where the mountains merge into the valley of Hsinteng County. The long row of cottages and houses that forms the hamlet runs north and south along the valley shaded by many trees. At the southern end is a watermill and the chuck-chuck of its pestles makes a pleasant break in the stillness of the country day. On one side of the hamlet runs a river through fields of wheat and mulberry trees. Beyond stretches a narrow plain to hills of red rocks and green scrub. On the other side of the hamlet runs a small stream through paddy fields that in the topsy-turvy world of reflection mirror the houses and cottages, their background of mountains and the dome of the blue sky. In the spring evenings, this mirror gradually darkens and the gay tones of the sunlit hours turn to dark and often tragic colours as the sun sinks behind the mountains in a blaze of strange tints.

But there was little happiness in this place before the liberation. It was a dog-eat-dog life. The biggest hound was Landlord Yuan. He had a thousand *mou* of fields, good, rich irrigated fields in the valley and hundreds of *mou* of forests in the hills. He owned several houses and a mansion in Hsinteng county town. He did no work himself; his "running-dogs," the agents, did his dirty work for him, squeezing out the peasants' life blood and turning it into wealth for him. Peasants who worked for him told of his fabulous way of life. He dressed in soft cool silk in summer; in winter his patterned brocaded coat was lined with sable, and wherever he went in the big house a servant carried a fire to warm him. He ate meat and fish every day. Rare dishes, like shark's fin and birds'-nest soup, were brought to him from Hangchow. He drank nothing but fragrant *Lung Ching* tea. A lot of what was wrung from the peasants stuck to the palms of his agents, but there was so much left that he didn't notice what went in squeeze.

His running-dogs were relentless hunters after gain. Nothing slipped through their fingers, not even the smallest cash. They treated the hired labourers and poor tenant peasants like curs, to be whipped, beaten, cursed and kicked.

Wong Kuan-yu, three years old, bare-footed, bare-backed, bare-headed and bare-bottomed, used to run and hide as soon as he saw them coming.

Kuan-yu's father was not even a tenant farmer. All he possessed besides the clothes he and his family stood up in and the rags they covered themselves with at nights in their hovel of a home, were a hoe and a rake and a few other home-made wooden implements. Like the rest of the landless members of the Wong clan he farmed in turn the five and a half *mou* of land attached to the ancestral temple. But this was not an unmixed blessing. If you farmed this wretched land you also had to pay the Kuomintang grain tax on it and give the two clan feasts at Ching Ming and mid-July. A horde of descendants of the ancestors would descend on the feasts and in a thrice the food would be gone. Precious little would be left from all the toil put into the ancestral earth. It was wretched land. No one was interested in improving it with fertilizer or even in keeping it in condition, so it got steadily worse as the years rolled by.

Lao Wong was always so perpetually hard up anyway that he often rented out his turn before it was due. Then he was reduced to the produce from the other five *mou* of public land attached to the shrine of the God of the Hamlet which he was allowed to till but not allowed to rent out or sell. This was a wise provision of the ancestors because otherwise it too would have gone the way of all else Lao Wong possessed — into the pockets of the landlord kinsmen of the Wong clan.

This five *mou* was poor, stony soil on the hillside and a couple of worked-out fields in the valley. If you tilled it you would also have to take care of the ceremonies at the shrine, give the annual feast for the villagers and pay the Kuomintang grain tax on it. What with all the trouble it involved, only paupers like Lao Wong cared to cultivate such land.

Lao Wong's life was a never ending struggle for existence. In his youth and middle age he had supported his aged parents until slow starvation snuffed out their lives. It was only when he was fifty that he could afford to get married and raise a family of his own, sons to cherish his old age. His first-born came in 1921, the year of the great drought that wiped out a good part of the crops and the lives of many peasants. Then there was another son and a daughter. Little Kuan-yu was born in 1932.

He knew little of his father. Memories remain of a brown, kind, wrinkled face; of fingers bent with cold; calloused hard from work with hoe and mattock, but delicately caressing as they stroked his head. Of little titbits, of turnip tops, soft and juicy with a pinch of soya sauce — a rare treat — pushed into his mouth at the end of a pair of chopsticks held in those hands.

Worry drove Lao Wong mad. When exactly it happened, no one knew. Something seemed suddenly to go snap in his head.

He had a cousin, Wong Shu-pei, who was rich, a landlord living in a big, white-walled mansion at the south end of the hamlet. He was a bull-necked tyrant who treated Lao Wong like dirt beneath his feet and never saw him but feared he was going to be asked for a loan. Lao Wong

in his part never saw him but he thought of the injustice
of fate that had let this white-handed, hard-hearted Wong
be born in a mansion, while he, Lao Wong, lived like a cur
in a hut that was little better than a kennel.

Lao Wong had indeed got loans from this cousin, loans
that tore the shirt from off his back, and took the food
from out the mouths of his children. Loans that had him
toiling from dawn to dusk on the landlord's fields, working
off, not the loan, but the mounting burden of interest.
Loans that finally set his whole family toiling, digging
ditches, fetching and carrying wood and water, cleaning
and chopping, hoeing and raking; compelled to give up
even his excrement to fertilize the fields of the landlord.
Madness seized him. He went to the landlord's mansion,
made his way calmly, with the cunning of madness, into
the house, into the great hall where the tablets of the ancestors stood, sprang onto the altar and smashed, smashed
everything that his hands could lay themselves on, cursing
the ancestors of tyrants!

Of course they caught him; beat him like a mad dog;
tied him up and let him lie in his blood till he came back
to consciousness.

He recovered his wits somewhat. He could work, but
when the spells of madness came on him he spent his days
gazing unseeingly before him. But he was always conscious of the children, always tender with them, especially
with little Kuan-yu.

He died in 1937, when Kuan-yu was five.

Life took its bitter course. Things were even a little
easier for the family; it was so obviously destitute and
worthless. There was nothing left to take from it, so the
landlord wolves lost interest in it. Elder Brother Wong
even got a job after a while looking after a landlord's goats
and buffaloes. He brought home leavings from the landlord's table for his mother and younger brothers and sister
to eat. They mortgaged their chance to till the ancestral

land each year and eked a living out by cutting firewood and digging up wild vegetables in the hills. In their best year they succeeded in living on what they could grow or forage for nine months in the year. They borrowed and begged to keep themselves alive over the other three.

Then came the time when Elder Brother himself wanted to get married, and he did, despite his cautious mother's advice. The warnings were soon justified. This brawny young peasant who was old enough to get married must be old enough to get something out of! He began to attract greedy eyes.

In 1945 the *pao* head had him marked down for service in the Kuomintang army.

Someone overheard the decision, gave a friendly tip-off, and Elder Brother made good his escape in the nick of time just before the usual New Year féstival round-up by the Kuomintang pressgangs.

Despair seized the family. It broke his mother's heart and she died just one day before he came back. There was not a thing in the house left worth selling. There was no help for it but to go to the landlord he had worked for and kowtow on bended knees and beg for a few dollars to bury her.

Hardly had this sorrow begun to fade in memories already crowded with care than the warning went out that the Kuomintang was organizing a big expedition against the Communists and was going to round up more conscripts.

Wong Kuan-yu's two elder brothers and other young men in the hamlet twisted themselves straw sandals, took a pot or two for cooking and fled to the hills where the roadless undergrowth covered their tracks.

Kuan-yu was left alone with his sister-in-law to look after him. He was thirteen now, small but strong looking. He found a "good" landlord, Yao, who, after much begging, finally allowed him to work as a buffalo boy. He slept with the friendly buffaloes, ate scraps left over in the kitchen and was promised 20 catties of rice for a year's work that was worth 500.

When he wasn't looking after the animals he helped the farm labourers and learnt to do farming. Three years later, a willing worker and a careful cultivator, he was offered a wage of 200 catties a year by another "good" landlord. But when he went to get paid off from his old employer he found he was in debt to him! It mattered not a bit that he was getting only a fraction of the normal wage because "he was too small." His benefactor demanded more work from him to pay off the debt.

The net of landlord exploitation closed in around him. If he went off without permission could he really hope to argue his case in the Kuomintang court? Furthermore the *pao* head, in league with the landlord, had already reported his age as nineteen instead of sixteen. Now he was eligible for conscription. More and more men were being pressganged every year to "fight the Communist bandits." This hung as a constant threat over his head and there was nothing with which he could bribe himself off.

Then suddenly the net was ripped apart. The Communists themselves came to Chekiang. The People's Liberation Army swept like a cleansing tide through the county in the spring of 1949. The Kuomintang troops fled helter-skelter. The landlords suddenly became less hard and stubborn. The *pao* head became ingratiating. But they only slightly loosened their grip on the peasants, as if they were biding their time. As indeed they were.

The main forces of the people's army had driven on south in pursuit of the retreating Kuomintang. Only that handful of revolutionary workers were stationed in the district. The hills about the county were still alive with Kuomintang bandits, stragglers from the beaten army and the landlords' "peace preservation corps." There were sporadic engagements as the Kuomintang bandits attacked and the revolutionary cadres defended themselves. It was an urgent task to mobilize the people and form a reliable force of people's militia which could protect the rear of the people's army until it could detach troops to complete the mopping up of the reactionary forces. The Communist Party called on the most exploited section of the people — the landless labourers and poor peasants — to defend the revolutionary order.

Wong Kuan-yu was one of the first to join the new people's militia.

True to the Party's policy of relying on the masses, the revolutionary workers chose to live with the poorest of the peasants. The young comrade who was charged with organizing the peasants' association lived in Kuan-yu's home and of an evening when the day's work was done he would tell him about the Communist Party, the people's army, and what the new people's government was aiming to do. Kuan-yu didn't understand all of this, but one thing was clear: for the first time in China, the people, the poor people, the workers, peasants, all the good people had united and overthrown those who kept them down like curs. The people had set up their very own government.

No picture had ever hung on the wall of Lao Wong's hovel. Now Wong Kuan-yu, his son, put up a picture: the portrait of the man who was leading the people of China in this great struggle — Mao Tse-tung.

Kuan-yu joined the people's militia, shouldered a gun and went to hunt the running-dogs of the landlords in the hills. Some were killed, some surrendered and others slunk back to their homes in secret. The people's power was victorious.

Kuan-yu, gay eyes, wide mouth, ever ready to break into a smile, became a group leader of militia. Second Elder Brother became chairman of the local peasants' association. Step by step they went forward with the revolutionary tide that swept clean the county and the hamlet. The Wong brothers took an active part in the campaign to topple the local tyrant's power. At the meeting where "His Fatness" landlord Yao was accused, he was brought to the meeting place and stood before his accusers by his own former buffalo boy. Kuan-yu told the full story of his meanness and bad faith and here finally before a just court, a court of the people, Yao the tyrant was made to pay up what he owed his workers.

In the three tumultuous weeks of the land reform, the power of the landlords was crushed for ever. Their land and animals, surplus houses and farm tools were taken from them and given to those whom they had formerly exploited and robbed with impunity. Wong Kuan-yu, made sharp-eyed against the enemy through years of bitter suffering at their hands, was made commissioner in charge of

grain requisitioned from the landlords. He saw to it that all that was taken was delivered into safe keeping and stored for final distribution to the peasants.

The sons of Lao Wong received seventeen *mou* of land and a room of the landlord's house. Lao Wong could rest in peace. Historic justice had been done.

Wong Kuang-yu

I met Wong Kuan-yu in the building which the people's government district office shares with the district committee of the Communist Party. Kuan-yu, now twenty-three years old, was secretary of the district committee and responsible to the Party for work in an area of over 17,000 people. He is happily married with a charming wife. She is chairman of the district women's federation. They have a new baby.

In those five years he had been trained and tested by the Party. He applied for membership and was accepted at the time of the land reform. Life changed with startling rapidity. He who had had to exert all his native wit and ingenuity to escape the ingenious clutches of the landlords, now had to learn to think as the servant of the people, solicitous of every aspect of their lives and welfare. He was an eager student.

He had learnt to read when he was young. His brothers, illiterate themselves but with all the ancient Chinese respect and love of learning, had scraped and starved so that he could go to school for a few months and that at least one in the family should be a "scholar." But when he went to toil for the landlord almost all this little learning had been driven out of his head. Now, like a hungry man before a table laden with food, he began to read all that he could lay his hands on to learn more about the party of the people, the Communist Party. Gradually the forgotten characters came back to mind.

As a cadre of the district committee he was sent out on specific short term tasks to various mutual-aid teams and co-op farms of the area. He learnt to carry them out with good sense and initiative. In 1952 at the annual meeting of county cadres he was cited for good work, and that winter he was appointed secretary of the district committee.

Kuan-yu is no very heroic looking figure as he stands in the courtyard in his cotton-padded suit. It is a new suit made for the New Year festival and it is a bit too big for him. Because later it will be washed and will shrink, it was made with plenty of give; meanwhile he has to turn his sleeves and trouser-legs up. He is just one of the crowd of young activists and cadres of the district, youthful energetic figures, merry and talkative when there's no work to be done, serious and concentrated when they listen, notebooks in hand, to a serious matter being discussed. Like the other cadres he lives in Spartan simplicity. He gets wages that give him about the same standard of living as the ordinary peasant. This oneness with the people is his very merit. When you ask the peasants what they think of him, they'll answer with a look of surprise: "Why, he's one of us!"

His senior comrades describe him as modest, willing to accept criticism, perhaps a trifle slow in grasping new things and not flexible enough in an urgent situation, but always devoted to his work and the cause of the people.

I lived with Kuan-yu for several weeks. And for those weeks I lived with the work of the co-operative movement. Today his every working hour is taken up with the movement. It is his responsibility to see that the Party policy is correctly implemented as it advances steadily, step by step, to the goals set.

It is his responsibility to see that the experience of the best co-ops is passed on to the others; to see that the key points of Party policy are observed as the movement develops from stage to stage, and that always the "class line" is firmly held: reliance on the former poor peasants and hired labourers; alliance with the middle peasants; and restriction of the rich peasants with a view to their final elimination as a class.

He has learnt from the senior comrades the golden rule of "check work, and check again!" In spring he helps the work of planning, of digging out the productive possibilities of the farms. He helps to organize the emulation movement. In summer he helps to check the work of the spring sowing, to use the dog days before the harvest comes to solve current problems. In autumn he helps to distribute the farms' income equitably and wisely. In winter comes the time for checking the work of the past year, building new teams and co-ops, consolidating, overhauling old ones.

Every ten days he convenes regular check-up meetings of the district cadres and activists where they report on the progress of work, hear what Party advice there is on the latest tasks and study the paramount importance of keeping always in closest contact with the masses, so that the Party can always be informed on how things are going and what the masses are saying about this and that.

Wong Kuan-yu is typical of thousands of devoted young comrades advanced by the people to see to their affairs. He is typical of the modest young men and women who today form the new generation of the Communist Party in China's villages.

He knows everyone in the village and is known by everyone. Remembering the days that are past he is keen to discern the difficulties that the peasants meet, he is heedful of their doubts and worries.

Kuan-yu heroically shouldered his gun to fight for the victory of the revolution. Today he fights no less steadfastly with pen and abacus, with books and tongue, with theories of new farm methods and new methods of organization.

If today heroism is daily, hourly, dedicated service to the people, to know their needs, to help them solve their difficulties as they advance under the leadership of the Party along the road that will enable them finally to solve the problem of poverty, then Kuan-yu and his like are truly the salt of the earth.

The Spring Festival starts the Lunar New Year. In the villages of temperate Chekiang it really marks the doorway from winter into spring. In 1955 it fell on the twenty-third of February.

The snow on the mountains and hills was melting. The first green sprouts were pushing their way up through the moist earth of the wheat fields. The slower tempo of winter work was giving place to the bustle of spring.

For days ahead the peasants of Chengling District were preparing for the festival. New clothes had to be sewn for children and grown-ups; old clothes washed and pressed as if they were new; houses and yards swept clean, and all things on the farm made shipshape. Down by the streams you could hear the sound of the laundry mallets; in the courtyards, the swish of the brooms.

There would be visiting for three days; and every guest would have to be fittingly entertained. Stocks of dried soya bean-curd cubes were hung beneath the rafters together with salted pork, fish and dried vegetables. Good market gardeners had carefully raised winter greens in sunny, sheltered nooks. The hens and ducks and porkers had been marked down and were being fattened for the feast. Gift parcels wrapped in traditional red paper were stacked ready in the living rooms for the head of the house to take to close relatives. The womenfolk made sure of a good store of fragrant tea, for they would mostly remain home to receive visitors.

Food was prepared well in advance. All the family and guests have to be well fed in these festival days. That concerns the living. But in addition, on New Year's Eve, many of the old folk insisted that the ancient custom of paying respect to the ancestors be kept up. Then the table loaded with eatables was taken outside the front door, lighted incense sticks were placed on it and, as they burnt, firecrackers were let off. Thoughts turned to those who had gone before, who tilled the fields and founded the family and, maybe, built with their own hands the good house in which their descendants live. And young and old bowed low three times before the family board.

Some even put up the old New Year pictures of the God of the Hearth. But most peasants today, sturdy, self-reliant co-op farmers, put up the new New Year pictures — pictures of happy workers and peasants, of scenes of New China, new factories and farms, tractor brigades turning up virgin soil, the People's Liberation Army, Soviet specialists helping to build China's new socialist industry, model village kindergartens and clubs—pictures of the desires of the people that are indeed coming to be realized. The pictures of last year were taken down and the new ones took pride of place on the main walls of the living rooms.

On these free evenings neighbours gathered for a good old jaw about times past, present and future. As often as not the menfolk got together for a game of cards, and to listen to the excited exclamations and the banging of trumps on the table, you'd think high stakes were being played for. But gambling is over these five years past.

Gambling used to be one of the banes of peasant life. A man could be stripped of months of hard-earned cash in an evening if he fell among a gang of drunken, Kuomintang ne'er-do-wells. Year before last a few men began playing for cigarettes but the women came down on them so sharply that that was soon put a stop to. Nowadays, with a pot of good home-brewed rice wine beside you, imaginary "points" can soon seem as valuable as hard cash. On New Year's Eve I heard such excited cries coming from next door that it seemed the players must be throwing five-yuan bills at least into the kitty!

Festivities went on without a break for three days. On those days all doors were open, day or evening. There were highlights to look forward to. The dragon dancing had died out before liberation as the Kuomintang troops had seized the "dragon" and used the cloth that formed its body to make shoe soles. But we heard there would be a revival of stilt walking and we were not disappointed. New costumes had been made and the village boys were practising for all they were worth. There were some hardy veterans who led the way but many were out of practice and were stumbling along with the aid of helpers or long walking sticks. One middle-aged peasant smoking his pipe told me of the days gone by when he used to walk on five-foot stilts across the muddy paddy fields. In those days the troupes would act out whole plays on stilts. They weren't so ambitious this year. A cymbal and flute band finally announced the performance, and I, along with the whole village, rushed over to the district centre. The noise of cymbals carried some distance and we already found quite a crowd gathered. The stilt walkers clad in a variety of costumes were already on parade. First came a hero in a rakish hat and armed with a sword, then an ancient official and assorted attendants, a damsel, an old lady and a "crowd" of rather nondescript characters. These were all more or less traditional masks, but at their head walked two new figures: a young volunteer to the PLA with a great red rosette on his breast and a staunch old man, a cooperative farmer.

These all did a sort of stately pavan, composed of a march around and then across the big threshing floor, singly and in pairs, followed by a "grand chain." The more skilled performers then did various tricks — hopping on one leg, tossing and catching their weapons, and the *kai-lu*

with their bright metal ends that glittered in the sun.   All
this was repeated later when about thirty stilt walkers
gathered on the public square in Hsinteng county town.
It was a gay spectacle which promised well for next year
when a more ambitious programme is planned.

Then there was a flurry among the big crowd. The crash
of cymbals announced a new attraction: a lion dance troupe
from one of the townships. A tiny figure dressed in pink
and white with rosy blobs on his cheeks enticed a pair of
lions with "fur" of green moss into the county town. The
lions gambolled and frolicked, as they sought to get hold
of the ball of happiness which their little tamer held in
his hands. A crowd of children and grown-ups followed.
The children excitedly clambered onto the stage where the
performance was given, the boy turning handsprings and
cartwheels; the lions doing balancing tricks.

The holiday crowds were in no hurry to disperse. They
munched long sticks of sugar-cane, ate sugar-coated rice
cakes and sweets, gossiped as they met old friends. We
from Chengling District however left earlier than others.
We had been lucky this year: the mobile cinema was coming to us, chosen out of all the other districts, to give a
showing of a new film.

We ate supper and then hurried off over the fields to
the temple theatre at the bridge over the Sung Creek. It
was already crowded to the doors. The performance soon
began. First came an educational short: *Modern Methods
of Childbirth*. A trim little woman doctor is shown taking
a class of mothers-to-be, telling them of the frightfully
unhygienic ways of childbirth practised in the old society:
unsterilized   hands   and   swaddling   clothes,   bandages,
scissors. I looked round at Mrs. Hsu, the wife of the chairman of Hsu Kuei-yung's co-op who was sitting behind me.
"Were things like that here?" I asked her. She nodded
without taking her eyes off the screen, where, after the
short-lived happiness of the birth, the young father is tak-

ing a little coffin from the house — the baby has died of tetanus.

Then came a practical demonstration of modern methods. The midwife comes to a farmstead and helps the mother and father clean up house. She prepares boiling water, sterilized rubber gloves, and a sterilized pack of instruments and bandages. Again I turned round and asked Mrs. Hsu: "Is it like that here now?"

"Not quite as clean, but nearly!" she answered simply. It was an interesting and well made scientific short. It showed in simple animated drawings the growth of the child in the mother's womb and the process of childbirth. It concluded with scenes in a modern peasant's home and the final bonny result of the birth. The many children in the audience and young people took it all in very naturally. Those to whom all this was new knowledge frankly expressed their surprise and asked questions of their neighbours and relatives. It was clear that the villagers now are used to taking in new things. There is, I suppose, some holding back, some reservations on the part of the old folk, but those of middle age and, of course, the young people, all clearly take it in their stride.

Then came the main feature. This was a new film made by the Northeast Film Studio based on the now well-known short story, *The Proposal*. A young peasant deputy is entrusted by his peasant constituents with the task of asking the local government to help them build a dyke to protect their fields. But at the county people's conference another deputy also puts in a claim for a dyke. There are only enough funds at the moment for one dyke. A heated argument ensues but finally the young deputy agrees that the other's claim is stronger. The dyke there will protect the railroad as well.

On his return his constituents are bitterly disappointed, and he has a difficult time convincing some of them that he acted for the best. Things become worse when a downpour brings on a threat of flood. Desperate efforts are made to shore up the old dyke; at the very last minute when a break threatens and the water is already overwhelming the flood fighters, reinforcements come in the shape of the other villagers whose fields, sheltered by the new dyke, are safe and who have come to give all the help they can. The day is saved.

Next year the young deputy goes again to the people's conference. He returns wearing a gloomy face. For a time he parries all questions from his anxious constituents. Then breaks into smiles, ends his teasing: the people's government is going to help them build not merely a dyke but a dam and sluice gates as well. These will hold back the flood waters in the wet season and release them to the fields in times of drought. The film ends with the triumphal opening of the sluice gates and the water tumbling through into the peasants' fields.

The characterizations are excellent. The Hsinteng villagers with deep amusement recognized on the screen some of the backward elements who exist in their very own villages. There is the old peasant who thinks only of himself. There is the worried old chap who, overwhelmed with a feeling of his responsibilities, takes refuge at crucial moments in simply falling flat on his back and pretending to be asleep. They recognized too that they had just such young heroes as the young deputy who fought on stubbornly for what he knew to be right despite the temporary unpopularity he knew it might cause him. I looked over to the young district secretary, to the bright-faced and even younger secretary from Tumushan Village, to the young county vice-chairman. I knew that this excellent film was pouring new courage into their veins, new resolution into their hearts. We all left the temple that night feeling happier, the stronger and better for the film we had seen.

Outside the spirit of New Year was abroad. Gay conversations and laughter, bobbing lamps and torches in the darkness as the peasants made their way back home over the field paths.

What a contrast this was with the past when New Year night was a night of terror or drunkenness, when good men were afraid to sleep at home. The Kuomintang pressgangs were particularly active on such nights of family reunion. This was just the time to catch their victims. This used to be the time for the landlord and the usurer to press with bitter insistence for payment of debts. A time for feasting in the houses of the rich, for black despair in the houses of the poor. All that had ended now. Now New Year was indeed a festival of the new.

Stilt dancers in Chengling District

VI

EBB-TIDE AND UPSURGE

THE "COMPRESSORS" ROUTED

In the early spring of 1955 in Hsinteng County hope was in the air. Never had the peasants lived so well. Mutual aid and co-operation had steadily increased yields. Long-term plans were being put into execution to increase output still more.

The weather was all that could be wished for: days of brightness with warm breezes that seemed to draw the seedlings up from beneath the ground; cloudy days of light drizzles that kept them fragrant and moist.

Little did the peasants realize that "well-wishers" were about to descend on them.

The co-op movement had been advancing steadily throughout China. Between the spring of 1954 and the summer of 1955, the number of co-ops grew from 100,000 to 650,000; 16,900,000, that is, 15 per cent of all the peasant households in the country, were in co-op farms. In Hsinteng County 76 per cent of the peasant households were in co-operative farms. There were the four large collective farms. But these benevolent people were saying (and not only in Chekiang): "Not so fast! Don't rush the peasant! He's only just got the land he yearned for for centuries and you collectivizers are proposing to ask him to give it up and enter a co-operative! You'll create discontent. Production will suffer. There'll be difficulties all round and the worker-peasant alliance will be endangered."

"Anyway the peasants and cadres are inexperienced. Who will run all these co-ops and collective farms you are forming? More co-ops mean bigger demands for farm tools, and our industry can't provide them yet. There will be economic chaos! How can you organize collective farms without tractors? Study the experience of the Soviet Union and go slow for goodness' sake!"

These people oozed pessimism with the best of motives. They even quoted Marx and Mao Tse-tung to strengthen their arguments.

Outside China there were heard at the time other voices. Voices were raised in surprising quarters bemoaning the lot of the Chinese peasant. He was represented as being ruthlessly pushed into co-operative farms by hard-hearted bureaucrats who cared only for the magic of soaring figures and nothing for the poverty-stricken peasant. He was described as being so much in love with his little plot of land that he would rather starve on it, sell all his goods to keep it and finally sell the land itself in the sacred cause of preserving private property.

This was the story bruited about the international rumour market by the "Voice of America."

On the one hand there were these cunning rogues who wanted to blacken Red China by proving that the peasants were being driven pell-mell into co-op farms, and that this was causing chaos and famine, etc., etc. . . . If it should have no other result but to stir up unfriendly feelings about China and perhaps slow down the co-operative movement, these gentlemen would be satisfied.

On the other hand there were the sincerely well-meaning but so misguided ones who saw only the difficulties of co-operation, who heard only the voices of the most backward elements in the countryside, those who were afraid of new things, who clung to the old ways and ignored the clamant demands of the mass of peasants learning to see in co-operation the road to the prosperous future.

It was some of these misguided ones who, in April, came down to Chekiang to inspect things and by a strange conjunction of circumstances, flaunting "the authority of Peking," were able to override the provincial Party committee comrades and set afoot a policy of "drastic compression" of the co-operative movement in Chekiang.

The months of April and May saw a struggle between co-operators and "compressors." And the lesson of that struggle has sunk deep in the soul of every contestant.

When the Hsinteng County Party committee was told by the provincial authorities, acting under the influence of these compressors, that it was going too fast with the co-operative movement, it demurred and argued back with facts and figures. But it was overborne in theoretical argument and it could not of course claim a completely clean bill of health. Several of the leading comrades had taken part in the events of 1953 when there had been that rush by the peasants and cadres to form co-op farms. They had admitted then that they had grown "dizzy with success," had in fact been guilty of bossiness and allowed some peasants to be pressured into joining co-ops. That was point one against them. And they couldn't deny that there had been cases of bossiness even now, and that there had in fact been cases of dissatisfaction in some co-operatives. That was point two.

The "compressors" declared that the facts proved that certain middle peasants had doubts about staying in the co-op farms, that others had complained that they had not been paid enough or promptly enough for the animals or implements they'd brought into the co-ops and that since some 70 per cent of the peasants of the county were now "middle peasants," this backed up their argument that "the peasants were discontented" and that "the worker-peasant alliance was in danger."

"Chekiang Province," so ran their argument, "was like a man riding a tiger and who couldn't get off. It must get off this 'tiger' of runaway co-operation or there would be serious trouble."

These arguments, of course, were specious. There were, it is true, legitimate grievances on the part of quite a number of peasants. These stemmed from various causes such as the bossiness we've mentioned. In other cases, carried away by the over-enthusiastic, some co-ops had, for instance, voted to sell more grain to the state than they could well afford. Not wanting to go back on their word the shortsighted enthusiasts had urged members to strain to fulfil their promised quotas. And some peasants had in fact sold so much that by the spring they regretted it and complained and wanted to buy grain back. But such instances were not difficulties inherent in co-operative farming. They could swiftly be remedied.

The main fallacy of the arguments for "compression" was that they were based on a partial analysis of the facts. They took a few isolated cases as typical of the situation as a whole. They lumped the peasants all into one undifferentiated mass, forgetting that poor peasants, middle peasants and well-to-do middle peasants (upper middle peasants, as they are called sometimes) in the co-ops each have their special interests and problems as well as common interests and problems.

The mass of poor peasants in Hsinteng, now they had got the hang of it, were all for co-operation. They knew it was the only way forward for them.

The mass of middle peasants, as we have seen, were not much better off than the poor peasants before liberation; they waver a bit perhaps at the demands which the new social organization makes on them—they do indeed have a deep attachment to their little plots of land and such liberty of action as poverty enabled them to enjoy—but as soon as the co-ops get going, yields increase and give them an income as big as or more than they got before with their individual efforts, they quickly settle down. Since they usually have some implements, and even draught animals and a little capital the combined efforts of poor peasants and middle peasants can soon put a co-op on its feet.

It is often more difficult to win over the well-to-do middle peasant. By his nature he is more of an individualist. He is not so keen on co-operation until he has been convinced and convinced again of its advantages, until it can really make his life better than it was before. It is important to win him over because apart from other things he can bring more draught animals and implements into the co-op and is a mine of valuable farming experience. When the co-op runs up against difficulties however he almost naturally puts them down at first to the co-op movement itself, and gets discouraged.

When there were difficulties with the grain sales, for instance, not a few of the well-to-do middle peasants took advantage of the situation to demand that grain be sold back to them just "in case" though they really did not need it; and of course there were some doubtful characters who did the same just to stir up the muddied waters.

When there is talk about the "peasants" say this or demand that, it's always best to see exactly what kind of peasant it is that is speaking.

It was true that at the time some 70 per cent of the peasants in the county were "middle peasants" but this wasn't the whole story. The vast majority of these were *new* middle peasants—poor peasants before liberation whom the land reform, mutual aid and co-operation and the people's government had enabled to become as prosperous as middle peasants. They were still, the bulk of them, poor peasants at heart with the interests and outlook of poor peasants. They had joined the co-op movement with enthusiasm. Only a handful of them had adopted the individualist way of life and outlook of the more backward of the well-to-do middle peasants. Only a most superficial analysis could lead one to think of these men and women who had advanced staunchly step by step up the ladder of co-operation, as "middle peasants" who were afraid of collectivization.

The truth of the matter was that the voices that were raised against co-operation were the voices of those upper middle peasants, the well-to-do, who in the old days had an eye on the ladder that led to rich peasant, to usurer, to landlord. They were not numerous voices but they were loud, eloquent and insistent.

The misguided sympathizers who listened to these voices took them to be the "voice of the peasants." Those who obeyed these voices, overestimating the significance of these wavering elements, were obeying the forces which opposed co-operation.

These backward voices found an echo in far from friendly throats abroad. "Drastic compression" of the co-op movement in Hsinteng County was in reality playing into the hands of those who wanted to hold China back.

The provincial comrades argued against "compression" but instead of getting out into the villages along with their critics and letting living experience argue their case for them, they tried to fight the "compressors" on their own ground over the debating table—and lost the argument, becoming as subjective in their judgement as their critics. They were overborne. The Hsinteng County comrades fought an unsuccessful rearguard action. The township comrades were filled with consternation when they received the "directive" for compression in April, but they could marshal no weighty theoretical arguments from the classics of Marxism to oppose the lavish quotations of the "compressors." They were hesitant to challenge the "authority

214

of Peking" which the compressors freely invoked—without full justification.

The Chengling district secretary Wong Kuan-yu was dismayed. Steadily over the months he had helped to organize the co-ops until 84 per cent of the peasant households in the district had joined. Now he got the message: "Compress! You've too many co-ops. They're too large. Disorganize them. Make it clear to the peasants that if they want to leave they can leave this minute and not at the end of the year. This is a crisis, ordinary co-op rules don't apply. If necessary, reduce the co-ops in size and numbers by persuasion. Let's hear the result."

None of the other district cadres could see the sense of it. It went too much against the grain. Wong reported back to the county, and got the arguments of the "compressors" thrown at him in an avalanche. Back in the district, he struggled with his soul. "To compress or not to compress? Was it right to go on arguing against compression against the county, the province, Peking? To compress . . . it hurt. But there must be more to it than he could see. . . ."

It is the nature of the dogmatist to be subjective, to stick to the preconceived idea in the face of the facts. The district secretary's views were ignored by the compressors who criticized him as one of those very people who had put Chekiang on this tiger of co-operation. He was ordered to go ahead and carry out the "directive."

He had argued his case and lost. As he said: "Now I curse my low political level. I should have been able to answer their wrong arguments better. As it was I was 'logically' convinced that I was wrong and that the compressors were right. But in my heart of hearts I knew it was not right." However now it was a matter of Party discipline, he took the "directive" and explained it to the best of his ability to the township comrades and co-op farm officials.

As the policy of compression was carried through a most confused situation arose. At first, as in many battles, there were losses and gains now here, now there, and it was unclear where the decision lay. It was a strange situation in which a Party member found himself actually arguing to hold back, or even to step back where before he had been calling for advance and again advance.

The ill disposed were not slow to take advantage of the situation. In the Yang Yu-chuan Co-op, one Lo Chuan-fa, who was later exposed as a former hanger-on of a landlord, had got himself elected vice-chairman and organized a clique of evil-doers who backed him up. At first, in order to consolidate his position after the liberation, he had "acted progressive," claimed that he had been exploited by his landlord patron and, as chairman of a peasants' association, had got himself classified a "poor peasant" in the land reform. By 1954 however he had grown more careless in the way he sabotaged the co-op; he began to browbeat members to prevent democratic discussion of things he objected to and even got one poor peasant critic expelled for "stirring up trouble." Now he got his gang to instigate complaints that the principle of voluntariness was not being observed in the co-op! It wasn't difficult! They raised chaos. For three days all work was dislocated. And this was at one of the busiest seasons of the year— transplanting the rice seedlings. Lo called a meeting and pushed through a resolution for dissolution. The co-op fell to pieces. From 107 households it fell to 11. The news spread through the district like wildfire.

Members of other co-ops wept openly when they heard that "the Party says co-ops should dissolve if they aren't run well, if they haven't enough capital, if the middle peasants are dissatisfied. . . ."

"We knew we'd have difficulties, that's to be expected, but difficulties like that are no reason to dissolve. We can get over them," they said.

But the compressors were adamant. Where there was confusion and dismay, they considered this justification for giving that dismay the final turn of the screw that often led to the break-up of the co-op. There were never more than a handful in any case who listened with any sympathy to talk of withdrawal, but once such withdrawals began they sometimes panicked other members and the co-op would be threatened with collapse.

Armed with this "directive" disgruntled members needled cadres into what amounted in some cases to compulsory compression. Where not enough attention had been paid to the interests of the old middle peasants and well-to-do middle peasants they were naturally among the first to withdraw. They took their draught animals and tools with them and these were in many cases the bulk of the animals and tools of the co-op, leaving the rest of the members—mostly poor and not so well-off middle peasants—in difficult straits.

The work done by the Party in the past five years however had been solidly founded. The vast majority of peasants held fast to the road of co-operation. No compressor could make them withdraw from their beloved co-ops. Those who did withdraw organized mutual-aid teams again. Very few went back to individual farming. Nevertheless, serious damage was done to the peasants' interests. The compressors caused them heavy losses.

Chou Yu-lin was a poor peasant whose only brother had been killed by the Kuomintang. Now he was the sole support of his mother. He had good cause to hate the Kuomintang and the hateful past it stood for. He became one of the foremost of the young men who gathered around the Communist Party in his village after liberation. Lithe, active, strong-limbed, militant, he joined the people's militia and became one of its leaders. He took an active part in the movement to overthrow the local tyrants. He was later admitted to the Party and was one of the first to throw himself heart and soul into the movement for mutual aid and co-operation. With a sturdy group of members, by 1955 the co-op of which he was chairman grew to 26 households. Twenty-three of them were poor peasants, one was a lower middle peasant and two were upper middle peasants. Their red earth was not so fertile as the good black earth lower down the valley, but they were forging ahead steadily.

Then in April a comrade came from the county town. We will call him Comrade Chao. He was twenty-eight years old, conscientious, young in experience but old enough to be a bit complacent about his abilities and a bit proud of the responsibility entrusted to him. He had done good work in a number of fields (and he is doing good work now too), but had been doing desk work for some time and was inexperienced in the practical day-to-day work of the co-op movement. Short-sighted and a bit one-track minded, he felt he had a job to do and was determined to do it to the best of his ability: to "mobilize" the peasants to contract their co-op farm.

Chao took a swift look round. Chou Yu-lin's co-op was not perfect. Chao had little difficulty in finding defects. He pointed out that it was not managed as well as it might be. He showed that it lacked capital to expand production. He picked on all the faults he could find. Instead of searching out the strong points of the co-op and consolidating these as a step to overcome the weak points, by overhauling the organization and methods of work, he used the weak points as an argument for a wholesale retreat.

But Chou Yu-lin was stubborn. He knew that practically all that the poor peasant members of the co-op had, came from the co-op movement. It was their life, their future that was at stake. "Compression" would throw them back.

One of the teams had complained that it wasn't getting enough work. Chao seized on this: "You've not enough

218

experience to run the co-op properly. Better let them withdraw!"

Chou Yu-lin demurred. Chao was insistent, thumping the table: "You're a Party member, but you don't obey the Party!" He made lavish use of well-worn clichés: "Your Party spirit is weak!"

Yu-lin knew enough to know that the Party never issues orders that must be mechanically obeyed, irrespective of consequences. The Party member must intelligently apply the directive to the situation that confronts him. If he sees that the order cannot apply, then he reports back. On the principle of democratic centralism, the higher authority then takes the responsibility if it considers that the order should still be carried out. If the man on the spot mechanically applies the directive and this leads to trouble, then he assumes the responsibility for his action and the consequences.

Chou Yu-lin checked with his members. They didn't want to break up the co-op.

"We'll get over our defects. Besides, the crops are ripening," he told Chao. Winter wheat, barley, and rapeseed were standing in the fields. "There'll be more confusion and worse trouble if people withdraw now. They'll lose by it right away."

But Chao was insistent: "If you go on like this, wasting manpower, you'll not increase but decrease production. Then you'll answer for it!"

He went away after hearing Chou Yu-lin announce as chairman that all who wanted to withdraw were at liberty to do so if they felt that they had not entered entirely of their own free will.

However Chao was unwilling to admit defeat. He came back a day or so later and called a general meeting of members—Chou Yu-lin was away at the moment—and this time had more "success." He managed to persuade Chiu Pei-yung, another Party member in the co-op, that it was his "duty" to set an example. Pei-yung announced his withdrawal.

The co-op was thrown into confusion. Chiu had been head of the peasants' association at the time of the land reform and the members had a saying: "If you want to farm better and live better, follow Chiu Pei-yung!" Now Pei-yung was leaving the co-op!

Chao poured oil on the flames. The nine members of the dissatisfied team withdrew *en bloc*. Confusion spread and seven more members withdrew. Influenced by the two well-to-do middle peasants who took back their buffaloes, the "withdrawers" demanded that all the commonly owned property of the co-op should be divided up. The remaining buffalo which they had bought in common would have been sold too if the young accountant from the county who had come to help them hadn't suggested that it be retained by the remnant of the co-op and used both by it and the members who had withdrawn but still needed its services.

Chao, highly satisfied, bustled back to the county town to report on the success of his mission and the correctness of the "line of compression."

This drastic compression left the eight poor peasants and one middle peasant who remained in the co-op in difficulties. The big pond that the co-op had been building to irrigate 50 *mou* of land had to be abandoned. As a result, that 50 *mou* could not be used to plant a double crop on as they had planned. Precious time was wasted. Co-op funds were depleted. The well-to-do middle peasants, who had withdrawn, had most of the spare capital in the hamlet. So there was no money to buy fertilizer. (Even the contents of the night soil pits had been divided up!) The compressors had also reduced the flow of credit from the People's Bank. The withdrawers sneered at the nine. But, led by Chou Yu-lin, they stubbornly carried on. They had taken the lead in the co-op movement from the start and were determined not to be swerved from their path. Chang Ah-yao's son was in the People's Liberation Army. He felt he owed an added loyalty to the co-op as a duty to him. "No backsliders are going to keep me from going ahead to socialism!" he stoutly declared. As in the Tumushan co-op in 1953, difficulties just put them on their mettle and they redoubled their efforts.

Small hydro-electric
power station at Chinho —

First they solved the water problem. They repaired some of the old ponds they still had and built a small new one. They realized all the capital they could muster down to their last coppers and bought locally produced fertilizer cheap. They spent all their spare time gathering grass fertilizer, making compost and digging up the rich silt from the pools and streams. Each man worked for two.

When the autumn harvest came they reaped a record harvest averaging 420 catties a *mou*, 12 per cent higher than in 1954 and 20 catties a *mou* more than those who had withdrawn so hastily from the co-op. They had boldly used the new double crop method on 20 per cent of the rice land and their courage and boldness had paid off. They got 600 catties a *mou* from this land by interplanting.

After the harvest is in comes a time for thought. Those who had allowed themselves to be "compressed" had a lot to think about.

They couldn't sneer away the fact that Chou Yu-lin's co-op farm had got a five per cent bigger yield than them, and there were plenty of other and even more convincing examples to teach them the same lesson.

In Yungho Township the Yung Chang Co-op and the ill-fated Yang Yu-chuan Co-op had planned to plant 500 *mou* with high yield late rice or double crops that year, but as they both broke up, in the upshot only six *mou* were so planted. That meant a loss, as the future proved, of at least 70,000 catties of rice to the peasants and the state.

This township suffered most from the compressors. The moral was pointed up by the Pao Chin Co-op there which refused to be compressed. It got its reward by getting a crop 20 per cent bigger than the year before. In 1954, their yield was 380 catties to the *mou*. In 1955 it was 456. The compressed co-ops failed to increase yields. They remained at 440 and 400 catties a *mou* respectively.

When the advice was brought to Chingho Township that their big collective farm—the pride of the county—should be reduced from its 318 households to three small co-ops, the Chingho cadres were roused. Comrade Chang, head of the mutual aid and co-operation department of the county Party committee, himself came down to explain things. But he got no response when he suggested compression. All the leading comrades of the farm opposed the idea. They pointed out that the collective, while not perfect, clearly fulfilled the basic requirements: all had joined voluntarily, output and income were steadily increasing. Such defects as it had were not the main thing. An overhaul at the right time would solve them.

Comrade Chang, duty bound, warned them: "Don't be complacent and conceited now! You'll have to make good on your pledge to increase yields and output this autumn. Anyway you must consult your members."

It seemed a shameful thing to take a proposal for "compression" to the members at this stage, nevertheless it was done. The members were unanimous: "No compression!"

Comrade Chang went back to the county for further instructions. He was followed by a letter to county and provincial authorities criticizing them for taking a one-sided view of things. At Chingho the compressors were forced to beat a retreat.

The other three collective farms in the county also refused to be compressed and nothing could move them.

The future fully justified them. Pien Chu-shen's Chingho Collective Farm changed 47 per cent of its land to the new method of cultivation and reaped a double crop of 606 catties a *mou* on it. It raised 37 per cent more grain than the year before. Previously this mountain village had to bring in 170,000 catties of grain from outside to eke out what it produced itself. In 1955 for the first time it triumphantly brought its carts loaded with a surplus of 35,000 catties of rice to sell to the state.

In Chengling District the Wang Wen-ken and Hsu Kuei-yung Co-ops also proved to be stubborn co-operators. And they helped the co-op movement by reaping record crops. In going against the compressors they felt duty bound to prove by deeds that their decision was right.

Wang Wen-ken's co-op put 55 per cent of its rice land to the double crop method. They reaped 524 catties a *mou*; this was 33 per cent more than in 1954 and the average income was 1,606 catties per person. Some families, like Wang Tse-liang's, got as much as 18,000 catties of rice. With a total extra crop of 60,000 catties they could sell more grain to the state and in fact sold 110,000 catties, 20,000 more than they had pledged. Before that harvest only two of the original 23 members of the co-op had bank accounts. Now 20 put savings totalling 800 yuan into the credit co-op savings accounts.

Hsu Kuei-yung's co-op, despite some wavering, stood firm. It too reaped a record harvest with a yield of 482 catties a *mou*, 18 per cent more than in 1954. And these weren't the best results either. Hsu Hsiao-jung's co-op in Chenlin Township raised its members' income 100 per cent!

Wong Kuan-yu, the young Party secretary in the district, had approached the task of "compression" in a responsible way. He reported to the local Party workers and co-op officials, explained the reasons for the suggested compression, got the inevitable negative response from peasants who had from the start spear-headed the co-op movement in the county, convinced himself of the true situation and the feelings of the rank and file and reported back to the county authorities. He was reprimanded by the compressors for lack of determination, but swallowed his medicine with the greater equanimity when these worthies themselves had to admit that the Chengling co-operators were standing firm.

It was just as Chairman Mao had said: where the co-op movement was led with warmth, vigour and method, good results were achieved. The district secretary felt deeply with the peasants of Chengling from whom he himself, a poor peasant, had come. He was sure of the eventual backing of the Party leadership in doing what he honestly thought was best in carrying out a difficult directive. He strengthened the hands of those directly concerned with work on the spot and who needed support in ploughing a difficult row.

As a result, despite the compressors, Chengling District continued to prosper. It increased its rice output 20 per cent, and changed a total of 30 per cent of its rice fields to the new cultivation system. The district was able to over-fulfil its quota of sales of grain to the state by 18.3 per cent.

Hsinteng County as a whole did not suffer as much from the compressors as some other areas, but even so the 76 per cent of households in co-ops was reduced to 65.5 per cent and the loss of grain was calculated at some 400,000 catties that they might have reaped if the co-ops' plans had been carried through. Total losses of course were bigger if all other considerations are taken into account. This is no small sum for a county just emerging from the poverty of the past.

Nevertheless the county as a whole continued its advance despite the compressors. It reaped 46,200,000 catties of rice, 4,700,000 more than in 1954 and its average yield was over 11 per cent bigger than in 1954. These figures were vivid demonstrations of the strength and vitality of the co-op movement in Hsinteng County.

Meanwhile the Chekiang provincial comrades had immediately reported back to the central authorities on what was going ahead. A fortnight later the answer came. Chairman Mao's famous article (actually a preliminary article that formed the basis of that later published throughout the press under the title "The Question of Agricultural Co-operation") was received at the very moment that the leading cadres in the rural work department of the Party were gathered in Hangchow to review the way things were going. It was a tonic. There had been little enthusiasm for "compression." Tired counsels of right-wing conservatives were not stimulating fare.

These worthies were insisting that it would take 15 years to advance to collectivization of agriculture in China. If 30 per cent of the peasants in the county were in co-operative farms by the end of the First Five-Year Plan, that would be enough, said they. Chekiang had already far surpassed that figure so what was there to do but to mark time!

In the villages, some of the people who had been among the most active were already beginning to think less of advancing to socialism than of how to prevent the well-to-do middle peasant members from grumbling and keep them satisfied even at the expense of the poor and the rest of the middle peasants. On the other hand the reports of comrades on the staunch attitude of the poor and lower middle peasants also began to come in. More and more light was thrown on the attitude of some of those upper middle peasants who had withdrawn from the co-ops. There were not a few cases where, while in the co-ops they had tried to get loans from them even though they knew they were short of liquid capital and were borrowing from the People's Bank, but as soon as they left they suddenly appeared to have cash to speculate with, lending out money at interest or hiring labourers!

And now came Chairman Mao Tse-tung's article. Its effect was like a bombshell against the compressors.

He castigated those who were "tottering along like a woman with bound feet, always complaining that others are going too fast," "picking on trifles, grumbling need-

226

lessly, worrying continuously and putting up countless taboos and commandments. . . ."

He pointed out that: "The tide of social reform in the countryside — in the shape of co-operation — has already reached some places. Soon it will sweep the whole country. This is a huge socialist revolutionary movement, which involves a rural population more than five hundred million strong, one which has very great world significance. We should guide this movement vigorously, warmly and systematically, and not act as a drag on it in various ways. In such a movement some deviations are inevitable. That stands to reason, but it is not difficult to straighten them out. Weaknesses or mistakes found among cadres and peasants can be done away with if we actively assist them. Guided by the Party, the cadres and peasants are going forward; the movement is fundamentally healthy."

He advised that: "The local cadres in the rural areas should be the mainstay both in establishing and checking over the co-operatives, and they should be backed up in their work and asked to shoulder responsibility. Cadres sent from above should be an auxiliary force; their function is to guide and help, not to take everything into their own hands."

He stressed that "many peasants are still having difficulties or are not well-off. The well-off ones are comparatively few, although since land reform the standard of living of the peasants as a whole has improved to a greater or lesser extent. For all these reasons there is an active desire among most peasants to take the socialist road. Our country's socialist industrialization and its achievements are constantly intensifying it. For them socialism is the only solution. Such peasants amount to 60 to 70 per cent of the entire rural population — this knowledge is already taking an increasing hold on the masses of the poor and not so well-off peasants. The well-to-do or comparatively well-off peasants make up only 20 to 30 per cent of the rural population. They vacillate. Some try hard to take the road to capitalism — a good many poor and not so well-off peasants whose level of understanding is low at the moment also mark time and waver. But compared with the well-to-do peasants, it is easy for them to accept socialism."

Gathering reports from all over the country and personally investigating hundreds of cases, Chairman Mao had analysed a situation that was typical of the whole country, though it had some of its most exaggerated effects in Chekiang Province. In fact he dealt with Chekiang Province specifically:

"With the adoption of a policy of what was called 'drastic compression' in Chekiang Province — not by decision of the Chekiang provincial Party committee — out of 53,000 co-operatives in the province, 15,000, comprising 400,000 peasant households, were dissolved at one fell swoop. This caused great dissatisfaction among the masses and the cadres, and it was altogether the wrong thing to do. A 'drastic compression' policy of this kind was decided on in a state of terrified confusion. It was not right, too, to take such a major step without the consent of the Central Committee. As early as April 1955 the Central Committee gave this warning: 'Do not commit the 1953 mistake of mass dissolution of co-operatives again, otherwise self-critical examination will again be called for.' But certain comrades preferred not to listen.

"In the face of success, there are, I think, two bad tendencies: one is that 'dizziness with success' which makes for swelled-headedness and leads to 'Leftist' mistakes. That, of course, is bad. The second is letting oneself be stunned by success, which leads to 'drastic compression' and to Rightist mistakes. That is bad, too. At the present time, it is the latter that prevails, some comrades are stunned by the hundreds of thousands of small co-operatives."

These words of wisdom blew like a cleansing, cooling wind into the troubled minds of peasants and cadres in Hsinteng County. They sounded a clarion call to action. It was too late to affect the planting, but they inspired the peasants to go at the harvesting with a will.

The English have an expression to describe a man who has to go back on what he has said, to admit he was wrong. They say: "He ate his words." The Americans call it "eating crow." There was plenty of eating crow that autumn in Hsinteng County, feathers and all! We Chinese call it "slapping one's own face" or in more modern parlance "stringent self-criticism," it's all one.

Ebb-tide changed to upsurge. When the peasants heard the news they were overjoyed. "We knew Chairman Mao could never agree to such a thing as 'drastic compression' of our co-ops," they said. They were also justifiably indignant: "Chairman Mao in Peking knows better what we want than you who live with us!" they scolded shamefaced compressors. More than one frustrated co-operator swore: "If this happens again I'll write straight to Chairman Mao!"

Chengling district Party secretary Wong Kuan-yu blossomed out with the broadest of his broad smiles. He had helped to stem what might have developed into panic withdrawals. His faith in the masses and the Party had been fully vindicated. He effectively publicized Chairman Mao's article and channelled the upsurge of co-operation so that it ran strong and straight to its goal. The peasants needed little urging, but there were masses of problems to be tackled to set things to rights. He fell ill but carried on buoyed up by the enthusiasm of the peasants which mounted to the highest peaks it had touched since liberation and land reform.

By November 325 co-op farms were all rehabilitated. They comprised the vast majority of households in the county. But as in every other part of the country this couldn't satisfy the new temper of the peasants. The popular cry was: "Produce more!"

Learning from their experience of the collective farms and co-ops they saw that this could best be achieved by over-all planning, changing over to the new double crop system, by ending the payment of dividend on landshares — a passive factor under the new conditions, and introducing the piece-work system — payment for work done only, as the basis of earnings or remuneration in the co-op, a system that gave the greatest stimulus to labour.

Farm after farm voted to press on to full collectivization. Between December 1955 and January 1956, the farms began to merge and reorganize as collective farms. By March there were 82 large collective farms with 97 per cent of all the peasant households. Most of the rest were in co-op farms, making a total of 99.3 per cent in collectives or cooperatives. Virtually the entire county rural population of 77,000 were organized.

The new collective farms number hundreds of households. Hsinteng County has 59 with from 100 to 300 households, five with over 500 and one of these has over 1,000. In Chengling District the 103 co-ops merged into 11 collective farms.

The peasants of Chingho Township had planned to try and get the whole township into one big farm by 1957. Now, with the enthusiasm that prevailed after the victory over the compressors and this record harvest, this was done right away. The 456 households of the valley linked their fortunes. A production campaign was launched immediately and as a result 70 per cent of the fields are being double cropped this year and 1,000 catties a *mou* is expected. The tea is being better processed and is commanding a better price; an 8 h.p. charcoal engine is being bought to mechanize some of these processes and for milling and pumping water; 500 more peach and plum trees have been planted. They have invested in the future with a new 7,000 yuan school building.

The immense reservoir of energy released by this upsurge and the new possibilities for creative work provided by the collective form of organization were skilfully channelled by the cadres into practical work. The masses responded to the call to "Produce More!" by a stream of concrete suggestions. "Only more production will make this 'kingdom of mountains and rivers' impregnable!" they said.

In the six months of the preceding winter and spring the peasants of Chengling District spent 80,000 man-days on water conservancy work. Now, in the three months from October to December, they spent 90,000 man-days building four large new reservoirs. That at Ta Lei-shan can serve 250 *mou* of land in case of drought for 40 days. Over 100 *mou* of hilly wasteland was planted to tea gardens. Better winter work ensured the planting of more oil crops to increase output 100 per cent. The area sown to winter wheat or barley was 20 per cent more than planned, and nearly three-quarters of this was sown in rows rather than in the old "clump" method. This is giving an extra output of 30 per cent this spring harvest.

Before liberation, due to feudal landlord rule and the individual nature of the farm economy, the irrigation system in Hsinteng County was chaotic in the extreme and among the most backward in Chekiang Province. Now, as a result of this new work and what had gone before in the mutual aid and co-operative phase of the movement, it was entirely reformed so that about 70 per cent of the arable land can defy drought for 40 days, and the remaining 30 per cent, for 30 days. This is of supreme importance in introducing the double crop and late rice crop system. This requires stable conditions of irrigation for success. Now it is possible to use 57 per cent of the land of the county, or about 58,000 *mou*, for double cropping, sowing two crops in quick succession. This gives the best yield. Another 20,000 *mou* are adapted for two interplanted crops, one of early rice sown in early May and reaped in mid-July, and the other of quick ripening late rice which is harvested in mid-October. In the past the single crop of semi-late rice which was the only one grown here, never normally gave a yield of more than 400 or so catties a *mou*. Now, by double cropping yields of up to 1,000 catties have been reached.

More manpower became available and the peasants worked harder and more skilfully. In the spring a socialist emulation movement started that brought more women out to field work than ever before. The Sunghsi Collective Farm formed of the Hsu Kuei-yung and Wang Wen-ken Co-ops merged with 29 other smaller co-ops; it has 1,225 households. Now 700 of its 900 able-bodied women have joined field work. The others of course do domestic work and side-occupations, they care for the children in the busy seasons, so they too do their share. Age is no obstacle. Mrs. Wang Ah-ying of the No. 3 Brigade is 70 years old but she says: "The older I get, the more interesting it is to be alive!" Last year she was awarded a brand new hoe for her good work in the fields. "I'll make full use of this," she exclaimed. "I'll wear out more than one hoe yet! We paid rent to the landlord. We paid tax to the Kuomintang. Why shouldn't I work better than ever now we work for ourselves!"

In the same brigade, there is a 60-year-old woman with bound feet. If she had gone out into the fields to work before liberation the superstitious would have said the plants would wither under her feet. Now she has joined the emulation movement and applies fertilizer to the plants.

These things are happening everywhere.

In the Chou Yu-lin Co-op those who had allowed themselves to be panicked into "compression" talk regretfully of their lapse and work harder than ever, to make up for it. Tung Shui-ho sighed when he rejoined: "This half year past we followed the wrong road. What time we wasted! Let me back in!"

A well-to-do middle peasant, one of the last to come back, admitted: "I'm not such a fool as to make the same mistake two years running. I want to rejoin!"

In no time at all the nine-man poor peasant co-op had grown bigger than before — to 49 households. Chiu Shu-ken put the seal on when he said: "This time we've really 'turned over' and there's no turning back!"

They completed that big pond they'd begun and then abandoned. They used the silt from its bottom mixed with compost on 80 per cent of their land. They worked day and night in sleet and snow to make up for lost time. Soon many other smaller co-ops joined with them to form an 800 household collective farm in January 1956.

Chou Yu-lin's grit as leader was commended and he was elected to the Party branch committee of the township. Now the big collective is one of the best farms in the district. Seventy per cent of its land is adapted to the new, high yield, double crop method. This is the mark of a good co-op in the county. They are in the competition to earn the title of 1,000 catty a *mou* farm.

Party and government have bent all their energies to the task of helping the movement consolidate its advance. A big problem was finance. Once, when a representative of the People's Bank came to a co-op in financial difficulties to see what could be done to help it, a well-to-do peasant member slapped him affectionately on the back and said: "Our problem's solved! Here's our finance!" This passive attitude had to be corrected. The People's Bank does all it can to help but the co-ops must rely primarily on their own resources. One result of the upsurge was the increased vigour of the credit co-op movement. In 1955 the bank and credit co-ops advanced the peasants 290,000 yuan in loans mostly for productive investments.

This was topped in the first five months of 1956 when 484,000 yuan were loaned out.

It is on the basis of such efforts and achievements that plans are being realized in the county to increase production this year by an average of 35 per cent compared to 1955. Everybody, however, is working to overfulfil this plan and bring the average up to 50 per cent. Individual farms have plans running from 50 per cent to 60 and 70 and even in one case to 100 per cent! And this after "unreal" plans sent for registration by the county authorities had been cut and made more realistic.

As they sit around the fire of a winter's evening or gossip in the fields at work or at rest, the peasants like to compose rhymes about their life and work. Most of them are about the co-op movement, about their confidence and hopes in it. Now in Lungyang District they sing this ditty:

Co-operation . . .
  a wonderful thing!
Wherever it grows,
  it fills your measure;
It turns the stones of the mountain
  into treasure!

HOW TO GET A THOUSAND CATTIES A *MOU*

At the foot of one of Hsinteng County's rounded mountains, where dog-roses flourish along the banks of the river, I talked to three little ragamuffins of buffalo boys. Sunburned as brown as imps, they cavorted over their huge charges. "I can sing opera-a!" shouted one in triumph, waving a home-made halberd such as is carried by the hero in Shaohsing opera. He put one foot on the lowered horn of his beast, and at the light pressure it raised its savage looking head so that its master could slide down its neck and sit face to tail on its haunches.

The two others, more serious, discoursed on earnings: "We make 450 work-points a year at this job. We feed and look after them whenever they're not working. We could earn extra work-points apart from that. But we're going to school!"

They came from the big Sunghsi Collective Farm, the 1,225 family affair formed of the merger of the Hsu Kuei-yung, Wang Wen-ken and several other co-ops. Their 450 work-points are worth a good 800 catties of rice. A grown man eats about 500 catties of rice a year. That is, these little men can already keep themselves in food and have a bit to spare. In the old days before liberation a grown man was lucky if he got 200 catties of rice a year and his keep for herding the landlords' buffaloes.

No wonder then that they rode off, bare feet dangling, completely master of their animals and with an air of supreme confidence in life. The "hero" sang opera. They whistled to the swallow that suddenly darted across the valley that was green with crops, ripening winter wheat, the tawny green of beans and rape seed, the glittering emerald carpets of rice seedlings, the sparse, tender shoots of transplanted rice.

These crops were their main wealth. It was on them that the value of their work-points mainly depended. Last year they gave an average of around 500 catties a *mou*; each work-point was worth 1.8 catties. Next year they will give around 1,000 catties a *mou*. The buffalo boys will be that much the richer. How is this miracle being brought about?

"A change in the relationships of production is transmuted into more rice because it leads directly to an increase in labour productivity. This is the key to understanding how output has risen in Hsinteng County. The peasants are using hardly any new machines."

This is what an official of the rural work department of the Party provincial committee told me as he sat at a desk of plain pine boards in the Sunghsi Collective Farm office (the former Chengling district government and Party offices) in May 1956.

Abstruse? Well, even such abstruse terms of Marxist economics have become common phrases in New China's countryside. But they are linked with practical, down to earth understanding of the realities of things. The rural work official recalled how, before liberation, the average individual farmer, peasant owner or tenant here, raised around 300 catties of rice a *mou*. Last year Sunghsi collective farmers raised 1,000 catties a *mou* on several *mou* of test fields on that same land. And they were using the same steel-tipped wooden plough drawn by the same buffalo, the same mattocks and hoes and sickles. But then they were crushed under the weight of feudal exploitation by the landlords. They could never manage to rise above starvation level so that they could save a little, invest some capital in their farms, diversify their farming and occupations, use better seed, more fertilizer, improve irrigation and so raise yields. They couldn't even use the water

236

sources available in a rational way because these too were in the hands of the landlords.

Now "the relationships of production have changed." They have freed themselves from the landlord yoke. They have their own land and gained the freedom to pool their labour co-operatively, and to pool their land so that land and water can be used to the best advantage by overall planning.

As we have seen in the preceding pages, they are now well on the way to solving all their old problems. Step by step, as they advanced through the work-exchange groups, the mutual-aid teams to the co-op farms, they have improved protection of their fields by building dykes or dams so that their crops wouldn't be destroyed by the floods or droughts that in the past periodically ruined them. This was the first essential. They also improved the whole irrigation and drainage system. They turned more dry fields into irrigated ones. Only co-operative labour could do these things on the scale needed to prepare the area in a short time for double crops or high yield late crops. Only the co-op farm could gain the necessary experience in rationalizing the division of labour and mustering and deploying large labour forces, so that the women members could play their full part in the productive life of the farm and, by providing suitable work for the older and younger people, free the fully able-bodied for the heavier and more important jobs. Only the co-op, spreading the risk collectively, could confidently undertake such new methods as close planting, deeper ploughing, rotation of crops, vernalization, and make really vigorous attacks on plant diseases and pests. It could also make more effective use of state loans.

The big leap, as we have described, came in 1955, when the farm discarded the old low yield, semi-late rice seed and began to plant two crops of quick-ripening rice either in quick succession or interplanted or one late-ripening, high yield strain.

The introduction of these methods demanded considerable preparation. The Wang Wen-ken Co-op's experience is typical. The irrigation system had to be thoroughly reliable. The fields had to be well manured and of even quality. This had been achieved as a result of the previous years' work. Team leaders travelled to see the new way of farming in operation at pioneer farms and experimental stations. Many evenings were spent briefing members on it. Finally the new seed was ordered. The supply and marketing co-op was ready with plenty of No. 503 early-rice and No. 10509 late-rice seed supplied by the state.

The new seed was placed in shallow tubs of muddy water; the heavy seed which sank was collected for vernalization and sowing; the lighter seed which floated was discarded.

The seedlings were given slightly more room than before in the seed beds. This strengthened them. The beds were slightly raised above the level of water in the seedling paddy so that, in case of freezing (for they had to be planted rather earlier than usual) though the roots were in deep mud, their stems would not be injured by ice.

Extra special care was taken in preparing, weeding and fertilizing the seed beds.

Ploughing and harrowing of the paddy fields was completed in April. The seedlings, now seven or eight inches high, were taken from the beds and transplanted into these soft fields of oozing mud, a few inches under water. All hands were mobilized for this task. It was completed in about a fortnight thanks to the fact that the co-op could direct its labour force wherever it was most needed. The planting was close — six inches between clumps compared to 12 before.

As soon as the transplanting was done, all hands were again mobilized to bring puddled fertilizer to the field and apply a big dollop of this directly to the roots of every clump. Women and the older children can do this work well, though it is no small task. Millions of seedlings nod their delicate stems in the paddy fields in May.

This mud fertilizer is a particularly efficacious mixture of burnt silt from the ponds, mixed with manure, compost and various other ingredients according to local fancy. It looks like chocolate and is kneaded with the feet into blobs as big as cannon balls. This the farmer takes into the paddy and breaks off bit by bit as he wades, mud over his ankles, stepping carefully between the rows of fragile plants. Potassium phosphate and other fertilizers are applied later.

In the weeks that followed the rows were hoed three times with the special rice hoe — a ring of steel eight inches in diameter attached to a long handle. A sharp lookout was kept for insect pests and diseases. Lime was dusted over the fields. Each team has a chemical spray now. Rice-borers and other pests were kept at bay with tobacco waste and DDT powder.

The first rice crop was harvested while the paddy fields were still flooded in mid-July. The fields were then harrowed and the second crop was immediately transplanted to be reaped when the paddies were drained and dry in mid-October. On 14 *mou* of land double cropped in this way the Wang Wen-ken Co-op got an average yield of 750 catties a *mou*. On 80 *mou* the rows of the first crop had been set wider apart and interplanted with late rice just before the first crop was ripe. These fields gave an average yield of 570 catties a *mou*. Since this second crop was harvested in September, this method seemed at the time less hazardous to the members, that is why, a bit over-cautious, they used more land for it than for the higher yielding "quick succession" method.

The single crop of late-ripening rice was planted on 120 *mou* and gave a yield of 530 catties a *mou*. This was harvested in October. It was the "quick succession" method that gave the 1,000 catties a *mou* yield on three experimental *mou*.

Fertilizer was carefully applied to each plant no less than ten times for the "quick succession" crops and nine times for the interplanted crops. Weeding was done six and five times respectively. It is obvious that only a well-run co-op or collective farm can do such labour-consuming work according to plan.

Wang Wen-ken, now vice-chairman of the Sunghsi Collective Farm, told me they were confident they could win the coveted title of "A Thousand Catties a *Mou* Farm" this year. He was sure that but for flooding and some damage from pests, the average yield for 1955 on his co-op would have been much higher.

This year, they are working as a production brigade of the big collective farm and so more effective measures have been taken against flood and drought. Dykes have been strengthened all along the valley. A big new reservoir has been built so that now 70 per cent of the farm's fields can defy drought for 40 days and another 7 per cent for 30 days. This means that the new methods of raising high yield double crops are being used on 90 per cent of the collective farm's rice land. Other land will be used for a winter wheat-rice-maize rotation. More land than ever before has been sown to winter crops — wheat and rape seed.

The transplanting and cultivation regime on the paddies will be based on the experience gained last year and will be substantially the same but more thorough. Sowing of seedlings was however 10 days earlier than usual in the old days. The big collective farm can afford to give greater care to cultivation. Every able-bodied man has pledged to increase the number of workdays he'll give to co-op work from 250 to 280 while women will increase their contribution from the 150 workdays of last year to 200.

The general income of the members will of course be supplemented as before by expanding side lines like raising more ducks, geese, chickens and pigs — and these will provide more manure. The big collective is building a brick kiln, a lime kiln and several water mills. They will continue making paper which has long been their main subsidiary standby. The yield of oil-seed crops will be increased by over 100 per cent (from 30 to 80 catties a *mou*) and of wheat by over 50 per cent by better seed, closer planting and better cultivation. All this will give a 60 per cent bigger output than last year.

And all this of course will again be coupled with that essential factor — morale. It couldn't be higher. In the big upsurge of the co-operative movement last winter, the whole township flowed into the co-operatives, their members voted to merge and turn their Sunghsi Co-op Farm into a big collective farm. Now all work is paid for on the basis of work-points — a piece-work system that is being perfected and that provides greater incentives to labour. The dividend on landshares — a passive factor as far as the wealth producer — the labourer — is concerned, has been abolished. The peasants are keener than ever to increase production. The greater the output of their farm, the more their work-points are worth and the higher is their income: this year it will surpass their combined income from work-points and dividends last year. The admission of all the former landlords and rich peasants to work on the farm means the elimination of all the "unorganized spots" that interrupted the land of the co-operative farms and sometimes made over-all planning difficult. Now the whole area of the township and even of the county is being planned according to an over-all scheme.

Truly, as they survey these wide-spreading fields of ripening crops, the collective farmers can say with pride: "This land is ours!"

The weather forecasts are good and so far things are going ahead well on Sunghsi Farm. Socialist planning and co-operation and the socialist enthusiasm of the peasants of Sunghsi will ensure that thousand catty yield and that in turn is the key to greater things in the future — mechanization over the next seven years, for instance.

Hairdo—

LANDLORD INTO PEASANT

Can you turn a sow's ear into a purse? Can you turn an oppressive, feudal landlord into an honest-to-goodness, socialist collective farmer? The proverb is out of date! The thing's been done. This is not a question of ones and twos, but of a whole class. This is one of the biggest jobs of conversion, re-education or brain-washing, call it what you will, on record.

By February 1956 practically all Hsinteng County's ex-landlords (and all its rich peasants) had entered the collective farms as members or candidate members.

In a little hamlet in the Shuang Chiang Collective Farm, where rustling bamboos put a cool shade about the office, Loh Ah-chuan, the former Kuomintang police-sergeant, usurer and landlord, told me how it was done.

The chairman of the farm, a poor peasant, whom his father had exploited and beaten unmercifully, sat by him with somewhat the air of a man introducing his protégé, and filled out the story.

In Kuomintang times, Loh Ah-chuan's father was a roisterer. Not a big landowner himself, he had only a few *mou* of his own; but through family connections he rented another 30 *mou* of ancestral, clan land, paying two per cent of the harvest as rent and sub-let these in small parcels to landless peasants at the rate of 50 per cent of the harvest. "A big fish eating little fish," the peasants said.

Most of the family income however came from usury and gambling. A loan of grain had to be repaid six months later with a hundred per cent interest. As proprietor of a gambling hell he took the lion's share of the money fleeced from the unfortunate peasants.

For this he could thank Madame the Generalissimo's wife. She was running a highly publicized "New Life Movement" and, with a flurry of trumpets had got an anti-gambling law passed that put gambling effectively into the hands of racketeers like the Lohs.

Loh Ah-chuan was his father's right-hand man and wielded the power in the village as Kuomintang police-sergeant. The Loh family snapped their fingers at the law themselves, but took the law with a vengeance to any "off premises" gamblers.

Occasionally Loh senior served as village headman, but in general he and his utterly disdained physical work. Work was for fools. Hired hands tilled their fields; a dozen servants were at their beck and call.

"We were scared stiff when we heard the people's army was coming," said Loh Ah-chuan. "We had a bad conscience. We thought the peasants would take it out of us. We'd skinned them unmercifully. Beaten many of them up."

The co-op chairman had got a beating once only because he happened one day to get in the way of Landlord Loh. There were few village families that hadn't starved because of the Lohs. How many peasant babies had gone to their death because of that landlord yoke? "Spring famine" was a yearly occurrence in this fertile valley.

Loh, father and son, were not surprised when they were arraigned before the local people's court as tyrants. But they were surprised that they got off so easily. They themselves had lived and acted according to the law of the social jungle: "Every man for himself and the devil take the hindmost!" They knew how they would have acted if they had been in the place of the peasants. Their vengeance would have been terrible and unmerciful.

Their fright increased as the long tale of their crimes was told by their victims. Everything came out bit by bit, even crimes they had thought were secret. Blackmail, extortion, outrageous usury and cruelty. The people had seen all! And even after liberation, they had hoarded rice and speculated with it during a shortage.

The sentence? — Restitution, where that was possible, of what they had stolen. Their land was confiscated but they were allowed to keep the house they lived in and as much land as every landless peasant in the village got in the land reform.

They got three years under public surveillance. This meant that they could live at home and go about their work freely. But they had to report to the local authorities if they went away from the village and they couldn't go out at night unless to attend a public meeting or for some other good reason. That was all.

The farm chairman added: "We followed the policy of the people's government: we disarmed the feudal landlords. They lost their political rights for a time, but we gave them a way to make an honest living. They had to reform themselves by working so as to become new men." A general policy of leniency had in fact been followed for all, even those who had been guilty of serious crimes if they showed sincere repentance.

Loh Ah-chuan was a bit constrained at first talking to a stranger. He was surprised that I wanted to know his story. When he understood why, he quickly lost his self-consciousness and talked animatedly. He has a long, rather angular face, is tall and strongly built. He wore a peasant's dark-blue cotton trousers rolled up over his knees — he had just come in from the paddy fields, and a well-worn, but clean and unpatched jacket of sky-blue cotton. Every now and again his face would light up with a smile. He would frown as he thought through some complex idea.

"We were afraid we'd lose everything and have to work," he recalled. "Well, we did have to work. We didn't know how to at first. We didn't know how to plough, or sow, or hoe or reap. The first few years were difficult, but the peasants taught us bit by bit, and we got used to working. We obeyed the orders of the people's government and lived quietly. Now we're not getting on badly."

"Last December I was admitted to the collective farm. I reckon this year I'll make about 2,000 work-points and my wife and son — he's fourteen and been to school — will make a bit too. We should have 5,400 catties of grain income left after we've paid up our share of the investments in the co-op. Before I joined I'd only made about 900 catties a year myself. So you see there'll be a big difference this year."

"The old man is in too! Though he's only a candidate member as yet." (A candidate member, the co-op farm chairman explained, has no vote on farm affairs and can't stand for election to any post. He gets paid for work at the same rate as full members however.)

Lo Ah-chuan

"And there's another big difference," Ah-chuan continued. "In these years past we've learnt to hate that word 'landlord.' We wondered when we would get rid of that label. Now this year I applied to the authorities to have my status changed from that of 'landlord' to 'peasant.' The collective farm is backing my application."

246

The chairman nodded approval: "There doesn't seem any doubt it'll go through. That'll be the end of that!"

Ah-chuan paused a while as he summed up his thoughts: "Now we can see again that the people's government is something new in governments. The Communist Party always keeps its word. The past is finished for us. Those old days were no good. It was wrong to exploit others. Now I earn my food by my own labour. I don't exploit any man. I don't wrong any man. Now I can look every man in the face and not feel ashamed."

The farm chairman smiled: "Yes, it's good." He summed up a whole social philosophy in the clearest of words: "If we are to build a strong, prosperous country, we must all work together. Nobody should exploit another."

How simple it all seemed! But I thought with renewed respect and admiration of the bitter struggle the peasants here had waged to gain power so that they could build their new life and in the pro-cess work such miracles as reforming their former en-emies, the enemies of society. I wondered too at the mag-nificent self-control and mercy of their actions.

Chairman of the Co-op

When Loh Ah-chuan had gone, I couldn't refrain from asking the farm chairman con-fidentially: "Are they really reformed, he and his father?"

The old man answered frankly: "Ah-chuan, yes! — That's why we admitted him as a member. He gets paid like any other member; he can vote, but for the moment

247

he can't hold any important post. Several co-ops had some unpleasant experiences when some of the old rich peasants and landlord elements got into the leadership. So we can't take a chance on that yet. But after a bit we'll see about ending that restriction on Ah-chuan too. He works well, and the peasants no longer have hard feelings against him.

"The co-operative movement here is strongly organized now. The peasants understand things well. Most ex-landlords and rich peasants are also not what they were. They know that all the rotten things they stood for are finished and done with for ever. That's why we're letting them into the collective farms. Everyone in our village is in our collective farm and we can make over-all plans for the whole township area. That's to everyone's benefit. We couldn't do that before and it held us back a bit."

"And the father?" I insisted.

"That's a bit different. Even six years isn't enough for the people to forget all the harm and wickedness he did. And we don't feel he's completely changed his ideas, that he's really one with us. That's why he's only a candidate member. He's getting on. He works. He'll finish his education in the farm."

So the Lohs and scores more like them in Hsinteng County were treading the straight and narrow. It was difficult not to: the peasants' eyes were vigilantly on them. With all the peasants in the collective farms it was well-nigh impossible to get hired hands to exploit. State purchase and supply of grain and other main farm commodities kept these out of speculative hands. In the towns the last avenues for speculation had been closed with the success of the movement for the socialist transformation of industry and commerce. All private industrial and commercial enterprises were becoming joint state and private operated while the handicraftsmen had formed co-ops. Now rehabilitation of all this flotsam of the old society had entered a new stage.

Cormorant fishermen resting

LAND OF PEACE AND PROSPERITY

The far-reaching social and economic changes that have taken place in Hsinteng County since liberation have now led to further administrative changes. Chengling District is no more. Collective farms comprise whole townships and overflow beyond the old township limits. Natural economic units today often overstep the old administrative units and so a complete reorganization of the administrative set-up of the county has taken place.

There were 32 townships in the county and one *chen* (the county town — Hsinteng). The townships were grouped into four districts. Now the districts have been eliminated and there are only 15 townships, and the *chen*. Chengling District which was composed of eight townships has been replaced by three townships. The political advance of the county is reflected in the steady growth of the Communist Party and Youth League. Every township has its Party branch or sub-branch and every collective farm its sub-branch or Party group.

Hsinteng County as I saw it last in May 1956, was a picture of prosperity. Green mantled the hills and valleys. The catalpa trees seemed like great white heads of cauliflowers amid the deeper greens of the pines, cedars and teak. Dog roses were in full bloom. Red azaleas made brilliant dashes of colour on the lower slopes. The trumpets of the yellow rhododendrons, shaped like tiger lilies, rose in rich clusters on their tall woody stems, beautiful, treacherous, poisonous. On the edge of brakes, grew purple, prickly royal Scottish thistles.

In the valley, the wheat and barley were shoulder high. Some fields were already turning golden. The deep green, thick-leaved oil beans were ripening fast, contrasting with the yellow fields of rape some of which had already been pulled up and laid to dry by the side of the field paths. The mulberry trees had put out their fresh green leaves which the womenfolk plucked and gave to the voracious silk-worms in their baskets carefully tended in thousands of warm, dry cottages. Men, women and children were busily engaged in the urgent task of transplanting the rice seed-lings from the close packed seed beds which looked like gorgeous emerald green Peking rugs, into the rich mud of the paddy fields. There was unwonted chattering around the state farms. Hundreds of cadres, from the swift limbed messengers to the portly postmaster, had left their desks for the day — May Day — and were taking part in the field work alongside the peasants. At this season of transplant-ing not a moment can be lost.

The primary school at Chengling had appropriated a length of the flat main road to hold their sports meeting. The middle school boys and girls were holding theirs on their new, flag-decked sports ground. The girls ran with a will, though with country modesty; in shorts, vests and blouses they seemed a bit overdressed for sprinting. But only a few years ago the very idea of this would have seemed utterly outlandish to the villagers. In the ham-lets, the small fry were aping these goings on. "Sports" was one of the popular games for a whole fortnight.

There was real substance behind this prosperous scene. More than 80 per cent of the former poor peasants of the county had now become new middle peasants. They live frugally, investing their money wisely. Eighty per cent of the peasant households are in credit co-ops holding savings amounting to well over half a million yuan.

Increased production and income has made the wheels of government run more smoothly. The state plan of pur-chases and supply of grain and other basic crops with its system of quotas fixed for several years, works well. The peasants know what they will deliver to the state both as taxes and by purchase and that the rest is theirs to dispose of as they wish. This stimulates them to increase production. All the 1955 quotas of sales to the state were delivered by January 1956, and an extra half million catties of grain as well. The plan for grain was surpassed by 18 per cent. On the other hand the state sold only 82 per cent of the grain it had set aside for peasants who usually needed to buy grain over and above their own production. Shortages of grain have ended in the villages. The peasants' tables are well laden. Their larders are full and each township has a well stocked public granary.

The shops are full of goods and doing a constantly expanding business. Unusual new goods are appearing. The centre display at one of the Hsinteng department stores is a harmonium, flanked by basketball posts, various other sports goods like javelins and dumb-bells and cycles and a 7 h.p. generator. Many farms are buying Diesel powered pumps and the county's first hydro-electric power plant of 20 h.p. has started to provide power for lighting over 1,000 lamps, for milling and irrigation in Chinho Township. Twenty-eight others are being built.

The personnel of the tax department has been reduced. Now the office uses the credit co-ops at the collective farms as its agent for collecting taxes (other than the agricultural tax in kind), this saves the peasants much time in filling in forms and making visits to offices. A single collective farm can save scores of man-days a year by this innovation.

Hsinteng County has its twelve-year plan. By 1962 field work will be mechanized. By 1967, last year of the plan, grain output will be 265 per cent more than in 1955 with an average yield of 853 catties a *mou*. Bigger crops of wheat and barley and rice will be reaped and more tea and tea oil, tung oil, tallow, rape seed and sweet potato. There will be more pigs, and sheep and goats on the green-covered hillsides. Geese will teem on ponds and rivulets that will be stocked with more fish. Three thousand five hundred hives of bees will bring more sweetness and wealth to the cottages.

There will be more schools by then so that 30 times more young people will attend middle school, a total of 10,000. Every school-age child will be getting a primary school education in 1958. By that year there will be virtually no illiteracy among the young peasants. By 1967 the county will have its own modern theatre and classical opera theatre and troupe, its own permanent cinema and 15 mobile units to serve the farms. All the main diseases will have been wiped out or brought under control. Hookworm and tapeworm, which are still a major pest, will be finally dealt with. The four evils: rats and sparrows, which devour the crops, and flies and mosquitoes will be eliminated. Now every township has its telephone and by 1958 every farm will be on the phone. Such is the plan of the Hsinteng people's government.

The sure foundations for a prosperous future have been laid in Hsinteng County, and not there alone. The whole of Chekiang Province is advancing steadily along the road to co-operation, to socialism, to prosperity. Practically all of the peasant households in the province have joined co-op farms or collective farms and well over half of them are in collectives. Practically all will be in by the end of 1956.

The increase of production of the farms more than outstrips the growth of population. And so far very little new machinery has been introduced. When mechanization comes and the country's growing industrial power is able to provide more chemical fertilizer, a further vast growth in production will be possible. Hsinteng County will be more beautiful than ever—a land without want, without ignorance, a land of science, abundance, democracy and peace.

POSTSCRIPT

In December 1956 just as I finished writing these notes, I received the following letter from Wang Chih-shou, the Party branch secretary of the big 1,225 household collective farm in Sunghsi Township which by then included the Tumushan peasants and the former Hsu Kuei-yung Co-op Farm.

Dear Correspondent Chen,

I cannot say how glad I was when I received the two editions of *People's China* in English and Chinese. Thank you very much for your kind thoughts of us. I read the Chinese edition and asked a college student who is now our agricultural technician to translate some of the English edition for me. All this makes us feel very much honoured. Thanks to your visits the successes we've achieved have been made known to many people in other places. Perhaps this will help those who don't yet know the happiness of living in a cooperative to take that road.

We continue along the road of socialist construction. We had another rich harvest this year. Our cooperative made 120,000 yuan more than last year. Ninety-three percent of our members increased their incomes. Eighty-five households each got an income equal to over 10,000 *jin* of rice. This made us all very happy. But we are not satisfied with this success. We are working hard to prepare for the coming year. All our members are hearkening to the call of the Party and the government to increase production and practice economy. We want to do this too, to support the just struggle of the Egyptian people.

My parents and I, Wang Wen-ken, our deputy co-op manager, and the children of Tumushan often think of you. Wishing you the best of health!

December 1956   Greetings from Wang Chih-shou

From time to time I received other news of Hsinteng County. In 1959, a group of students doing practical sociology there wrote to tell me that they had translated *New Earth* into Chinese as part of a projected history of the local commune farms. Hsinteng County, I was told, had been merged into a new, larger county and its peasants were all in a big people's commune farm formed by amalgamating several collective farms. Subsequent news has all been good. In 1969 they helped make Chekiang Province the national record holder for rice yields. They reaped an average of over 850 *jin* per *mou*.

People's commune farms in China are bigger than any of the old collective farms. Their several tens of thousands of members comprise production brigades (usually the former collective farms) which are made up of production teams (usually the former co-op units). The teams are the basic cost accounting units in the communes and are responsible for their own gains and losses. Naturally, the brigade or commune will help a team in time of need. In some of the more advanced communes the brigade is the cost accounting unit.

The commune is managed by an elected revolutionary committee that is, at the same time, the lowest level of government administration under the county and provincial local government revolutionary committees. It looks after the various activities of the commune: industry, trade, education, health and culture, military affairs, and agriculture, including farming, forestry, animal husbandry, sideline production, and fishery.

The commune as a whole owns certain large enterprises such as a machine-tractor park, brick kiln, coal mine, chemical fertilizer plant, iron and steel works. Since the commune is a state administrative unit, these enterprises are public property.

256

At the same time, brigades and teams own certain collective property (the main form of property in the commune) such as stables, draught animals, large implements. The peasant members have their own private property such as houses, small tools, domestic animals, pigs, chickens, and so on. In some communes they have small private plots. The work point system is used to calculate earnings. The old, orphaned, sick or disabled enjoy social security.

The new commune organization stood the peasants in good stead during the three years of severe natural calamities in 1959–61. Since then they have gone from strength to strength. They have established a number of stable, high-yield areas which during the last ten years have enabled the country to reap a bumper harvest each year. China now has no fear of natural calamities. Grain production in 1970 was 240 million tons. This was more than enough for the population of between 750 to 800 million.

A remarkable fact is that all this has been achieved by and large with the same basic tools the peasants have used from time immemorial: the spade, the mattock, the carrying pole and basket. Mechanization is only now starting in earnest. This has completely shattered the theory put forward by Liu Shao-chi, the ex-president deposed during the cultural revolution, that "mechanization must precede cooperation." Without waiting for mechanization the peasants have raised yields through cooperation. Liu was wrong because he failed to see what a mighty force is generated by the masses of the people working together with revolutionary fervor and according to plan. He failed to see that a powerful impetus can be given to the productive forces simply by changing the relation between the producers, by cruelly oppressed tenant peons transforming themselves into free producers, and, in the cultural sphere, by transforming themselves from illiterate, superstitious peasants into scientifically-minded collective farmers.

Liu Shao-chi's lack of faith in the peasants was also demonstrated in the events described as "compressing the co-ops." There I told how "people from Peking" had come down to Chekiang in 1955 and, arguing that many co-ops had been rashly set up, forced them to disband. At the time I could not get the names of those "people from Peking." Now, in the wake of the cultural revolution, I can reveal that it was Liu Shao-chi who ordered this "compression." Seizing the opportunity of Chairman Mao's absence from Peking, in May of that year he got 200,000 co-ops dissolved throughout the country. He never admitted this mistake. This book is so far the only detailed account of that episode.

JACK CHEN

Honolulu, Hawaii
March 1972